The Dying President

-
-
-
-

The Dying President

Franklin D. Roosevelt 1944–1945

ROBERT H. FERRELL

University of Missouri Press

Columbia and London

Library of Congress Cataloging-in-Publication Data

Ferrell, Robert H.
   The dying president : Franklin D. Roosevelt, 1944–1945 / Robert H.
Ferrell.
     p. cm.
   Includes bibliographical references and index.
   ISBN 0-8262-1171-2 (alk. paper)
   1. Roosevelt, Franklin D. (Franklin Delano), 1882–1945—Health.
2. Presidents—United States—Biography.   3. Cardiovascular system—
Diseases—Patients—United States—Biography.   I. Title.
E807.F4   1998
973.917'092—dc21
[B]   97-45797
                                                CIP

Designer: Elizabeth K. Young
Typesetter: BOOKCOMP
Printer and Binder: Thomson-Shore, Inc.
Typefaces: Palatino, Helvetica Neue Extended

▪ *Contents*

▪ *Acknowledgments*

Many thanks to the staff of the Franklin D. Roosevelt Library at Hyde Park, New York: Verne W. Newton, Director; Raymond Teichman, Supervisory Archivist; and Lynn Bassanese, Robert Parks, Mark Renovitch, Nancy Snedeker, and Alycia Vivona. Also to Duane A. Watson, Chair, Curatorial Committee, Wilderstein Preservation at Rhinebeck, New York, for the papers and diary of Margaret Suckley. And a multitude of helpful friends: George Canon, Calvin D. Davis, Hugh E. Evans, M.D., Alfred P. Fishman, M.D., Tracy D. Gage, M.D., Jeffrey C. Graf, William P. Hannegan, Jan Kenneth Herman, Thomas A. Horrocks, James W. Leyerzapf, Ethel McLeod, Patrick J. Maney, Donald R. May, M.D., Ernest Nalle Jr., M.D., Amos Perlmutter, David C. Voris, M.D., Peter H. Wright, M.D., and Sidney O. Krasnoff, M.D., who greatly helped with medical terms in the diary of Dr. Howard G. Bruenn. John Garry Clifford suggested changes in the text that proved very helpful. John Lukacs, the historian, proved a friend in more ways than I can mention.

Beverly Jarrett, Director and Editor in Chief of the University of Missouri Press, again supported this book with not merely her interest but her engaging enthusiasm. So did Annette Wenda, a fine editor, and Jane Lago, Managing Editor, who handles everything.

Once again a thank-you to Lila and Carolyn.

The Dying President

-
-
-
-

A half century and more has passed since Franklin D. Roosevelt died at Warm Springs, Georgia, and the date continues to hold meaning for the many Americans who can remember that stunning news. There are many more—they now outnumber survivors from Roosevelt's time—who have read about that day and seen the photographs at Warm Springs and elsewhere, the coffin being put aboard the train for Washington, the caisson passing down Pennsylvania Avenue, the West Point cadets firing the final volley in the garden at Hyde Park.

But the present book is not an account of a notable death, so faraway and yet so near, but an effort to look back at how carefully the illness of this president of the United States was kept from the American people. The president, it now can be said, knew he was suffering from cardiovascular disease, knew he was seriously ill, and chose to keep that fact a secret. Which is why, of course, the news of his passing brought such grief, for it was so unbelievable, so unanticipated.

New material has become available about Roosevelt's last year in office, especially the diary published in part by Geoffrey C. Ward in 1995, *Closest Companion: The Unknown Story of the Intimate Friendship between Franklin Roosevelt and Margaret Suckley.* The president's distant cousin, Daisy Suckley as she was known, was a pleasant-faced, inconspicuous woman who saw much of Roosevelt. She wrote everything down, and when she died in her one-hundredth year in 1991 her diary was found in an old black suitcase under her bed at Wilderstein, her house in Rhinebeck near Hyde Park. Other sources have opened, including the diary of Dr. Howard G. Bruenn, Roosevelt's cardiologist and virtually his personal physician during the president's last year. The papers of Vice Adm. Ross T. McIntire, surgeon general of the U.S. Navy, include a report by the Federal Bureau of Investigation of how word of the president's cardiac condition spread among physicians at Bethesda Naval Hospital and the Mayo Clinic, and of how the bureau moved to silence it. The materials for a new look at Roosevelt's illness are at hand. The huge book by the freelance writer Jim Bishop, *FDR's Last Year: April 1944–April 1945*, none too accurate to begin with, stuffed with irrelevant military and political details, needs redoing. Roosevelt's last year as it appears in Doris Kearns Goodwin's *No Ordinary Time: Franklin and Eleanor, the Home Front in World War II*, published too soon to use the Suckley diary, needs less nostalgia, more reality.

Another reason for a new account is the recent sensitivity to illnesses of the nation's chief executives, so evident in the passage of the Twenty-fifth Amendment some years ago. There have been too many presidential illnesses disguised by the presidents themselves or by their assistants for the purpose of staying in office. The notable first case of this sort of thing was the operation upon President Grover Cleveland for cancer in 1893 that took place aboard a yacht in New York harbor, during which physicians removed a large part of Cleveland's upper jaw. Reporters were told that the president had been suffering from a toothache. What really happened did not become known until 1917. In the years after Cleveland's illness several presidents became seriously ill: Woodrow Wilson, Warren G. Harding, and Dwight D. Eisenhower. John F. Kennedy disguised his Addison's disease, which was serious enough to have denied him the presidency, by refusing to admit he had it.

The final reasons for looking into the illness and death of President Roosevelt are the "what-ifs." The president's illness delayed decisions. In the summer of 1944, dramatically needing a rest, FDR arranged to travel by train and ship to Hawaii for a conference with his Pacific commanders, Adm. Chester W. Nimitz and Gen. Douglas MacArthur. The trip required five weeks, and the result, arranged in a two-and-one-half-hour conference, was a nondecision, that the U.S. Navy would continue its western drive toward Japan and the U.S. Army under MacArthur its "island-hopping" moves northward from Australia. That same summer the effort by Gen. Joseph W. Stilwell to galvanize the Nationalist Chinese government under Generalissimo Chiang Kai-shek came to an open confrontation, for

Chiang was more interested in fighting the Communist Chinese than in opposing Japan; Roosevelt gave in to Chiang and replaced Stilwell with a more complaisant commander. Not long afterward the president through inaction let the French Indochina situation, where the nationalists under Ho Chi Minh were beseeching the American government for support, pass back into the hands of the inept French government.

For the continent of Europe, FDR had no more solutions than for the Far East. The appalling Morgenthau Plan was drawn up at a conference in Quebec in September 1944. Acceptance of this plan that Prime Minister Winston Churchill described as the pastoralization of Germany, a proposal to turn the industrial heart of Europe into farmland, can be ascribed only to the president's illness. He was too tired to say no to Secy. of the Treasury Henry A. Morgenthau Jr., his Hyde Park neighbor.

Meanwhile, the "final solution" for Europe's Jews was in course, the most terrible act of the twentieth century, what World War II was all about. It raised an immediate question of destruction of the death camps. It was and remains an issue in which Roosevelt's presence has been difficult to discern.

During the last year of Roosevelt's life, as is well known, the president made almost no preparation for a successor in his high office. In a meeting a few days before the Democratic National Convention assembled in Chicago in July 1944, the president agreed with the party's leaders that the all-important (considering the president's illness) vice presidential nomination should go to Sen. Harry S. Truman of Missouri. He then wavered and allowed his White House assistant, former senator James F. Byrnes of South Carolina, to try for the nomination, which Byrnes for the obvious reason (the president's illness) wanted to do. After Byrnes's failure FDR nearly permitted the friends of Vice President Henry A. Wallace to stampede the convention; like Byrnes, Wallace knew the nomination meant the presidency, for Roosevelt would win in November and could not last through a fourth term. Wallace possessed virtually no political experience and could have been a disastrous president.

After the Chicago convention the president told Truman virtually nothing about military, diplomatic, or administrative matters. FDR did inform his successor in general terms about the atomic bomb, during a White House luncheon in August 1944. The next month he met Churchill at Hyde Park and concluded an agreement over postwar nuclear sharing, and not merely failed to tell Truman about it but did not inform his own State Department, and after the war the initialed document was discovered among his papers. After the president's fourth inauguration in January 1945, and inauguration of Truman as vice president, came the monthlong sea and air trip to faraway Yalta, and upon return the president told Truman nothing about what he had discussed and concluded there. Nor did FDR make the slightest attempt to inform Truman about the complicated workings of the American government, the vast array of cabinet departments and independent agencies that had grown by leaps and bounds during the New Deal and war years, over which the president presided in very personal ways.

And so the months of President Roosevelt's illness passed, with the nation's chief executive keeping his illness secret, confiding in no one. His physical abilities markedly lessened. A charitable estimate of the time he spent each day doing the public business was four hours, and was closer to one or two. His mind was unaffected; his problem was an inability to concentrate for long periods. Whatever his skills in the past, he could at best summon them for the moment. For the most part he let events take their course. He was, and it is saddening to say this for such a great historical figure, in no condition to govern the Republic.

1 ▪ *Guesswork*

ometimes guesswork passes for truth, and according to Vice Adm. Ross T. McIntire "rumor factories" in 1944–1945 were turning out false accounts of what ailed President Franklin D. Roosevelt during the final year of FDR's life.[1] McIntire should have known. He was surgeon general of the U.S. Navy and the president's personal physician. But it is an interesting fact that Admiral McIntire was himself a worker in the rumor factories, for at that time he was announcing a remarkably false account of Roosevelt's health. He was saying that there was nothing wrong with the president save influenza and bronchitis and that the president's health was as good as one could expect for a man in his early sixties.

Another piece of guesswork turned out by the factories concerned cancer. There was talk that Roosevelt suffered from stomach cancer. After the president died there was talk of a different kind of cancer, a malignant melanoma that in its beginnings was visible for many years in a pigmented lesion over his left eyebrow.

In a book titled *White House Physician*, published just after World War II, McIntire mentioned several other rumors. The president, he wrote, reportedly suffered at one and the same time from a paralytic stroke, a coronary thrombosis, a brain hemorrhage, a nervous breakdown, an aneurysm of the aorta, a cancerous prostate, and some people said ("favorite whisper of all") that his heart was worn out.[2] But the principal pieces of guesswork were McIntire's account that everything was basically all right and the false stories about stomach cancer and melanoma.

1

When President Roosevelt became a patient of Dr. McIntire, shortly after entering the White House in 1933, the new presidential physician must have thought that apart from Roosevelt's bout with infantile paralysis in 1921 his patient was in reasonably good health. The president did not possess the lean figure of earlier years when he was a legislator in Albany or during World War I when assistant secretary of the navy in Washington. He had taken on weight, and his face was full. But he had a healthy look about him. He radiated good health, even when—to avoid standing in his braces, which hurt in one way or another—he was sitting in an automobile that had been driven up to a microphone. The president's problems all seemed rather common. When a schoolboy he had come down with scarlet fever, and during the Spanish-American War when he was sixteen years old and thought of himself as a candidate for the army in Cuba he suffered a humiliating if unimportant attack of measles. He married his distant cousin Eleanor in 1905 and during their honeymoon in Europe endured attacks of urticaria, an inflammatory disease of the skin sometimes attributed to fleas, shellfish, or strawberries. His wife discovered that he walked in his sleep. He had typhoid fever in 1912, afterward remembering (FDR's memory *was* unreliable) that he had it twice. In 1915 he underwent an appendectomy and in 1918 after return from a brief tour of the western front came down with pneumonia. It was possible to contend that he was susceptible to illness, and his wife occasionally ventured that thought. She believed he was "much more apt to catch germs than I was." His immune system perhaps was not well developed. "When everyone had the flu, he would get it," she recalled. But then Eleanor Roosevelt was herself extraordinarily healthy and her judgment on this score was probably offhand.[3]

The infantile paralysis had seemed a terrible affliction. It occupied months and months of the early 1920s, as he at first required three physicians to diagnose his problem and then sought to make himself an expert in the disease so, he hoped for a while, to conquer it. The initial diagnosis at the family summer house on Campobello Island in New Brunswick was uncertain, made by a local physician. By chance the renowned Dr. William W. Keen, aged eighty-four, who had assisted in the operation for cancer upon President Grover Cleveland in 1893 and was a specialist in neurosurgery, was vacationing nearby, and Keen gave Roosevelt a wonderful misdiagnosis, a blood clot or a lesion of the spine, for which he charged the then outrageous fee of six hundred dollars.[4] A third physician, a specialist in infantile paralysis, got things straight. After a slow recovery from the initial severe paralysis the future president learned of the curative value of the waters at Warm Springs, Georgia. He visited the annual convention of the Orthopedic Association in Atlanta in 1926 and persuaded a committee of the delegates to examine Warm Springs, and in due time the visitors reported favorably. Without much thought Roosevelt bought the property and incorporated the Georgia Warm Springs Foundation, which included buildings and twelve hundred acres; he put two-thirds of his personal fortune in the venture.

Fortunately for Roosevelt the paralysis of his legs and thighs had not prevented participation in politics. In 1924 and again in 1928, he addressed the Democratic National Conventions, nominating Gov. Alfred E. Smith of New York for the presidency, and the second nomination persuaded Smith, who by then had enjoyed three terms in the governorship, to pass to him the governor's office. When FDR's prospects for the presidency began to be apparent in 1931 it was necessary to make some sort of demonstration that his health, despite the polio, measured up to the requirements of the nation's highest office. This he managed with aplomb. A Republican from Northampton, Massachusetts, the residence of former president Calvin Coolidge, challenged Roosevelt to undergo a physical examination by a panel of physicians, and he seized the opportunity. The director of the New York Academy of Medicine, Dr. Linsly R. Williams, formed an experts' committee of Drs. Samuel W. Lambert, Russell A. Hibbs, and Foster Kennedy, respectively a diagnostician, an orthopedist, and a neurologist. They reported favorably, perhaps too much so in light of the governor's obvious incapacities. They found his "organs and functions" sound in all respects, and said he possessed no anemia, had a well-developed chest, and a normal spinal column, "all of its segments . . . in perfect alignment." They added with information probably from the patient, "He has neither pain nor ache at any time." They remarked that the governor could "walk all necessary distances," whatever those happened to be, and "can maintain a standing position without fatigue." They concluded that he could "meet all demands of private or public life."[5]

After the inauguration in Washington in 1933 the president suffered a few minor problems, such as an attack of influenza in 1937.

Dr. McIntire in his book said the attack kept Roosevelt away from his desk for a week or so, "but he soon regained complete fitness, and checks on the heart, chest, and other vital functioning organs were satisfactory." (Interestingly, in one of the apparently few blood pressure readings made during the 1930s, the same year as the attack of influenza, the president's systolic pressure registered 162, more than mildly hypertensive and hardly satisfactory.) The president's personal physician said that he trusted "our Navy specialists" for checkups, now and then bringing in "famous consultants" during annual physical examinations.[6] Before a journey of any duration the president, he wrote, was given a head-to-toe examination, which was repeated after the trip. Such examinations continued into the war era, for the Casablanca, Teheran, and Yalta Conferences, the first two meetings in 1943, the last in 1945. On the examinations and checkups nothing serious turned up.

Meanwhile, Dr. McIntire was rising in rank from lieutenant junior grade at the beginning of his navy service in 1917 to vice admiral during World War II. The stocky, handsome officer was born in Salem, Oregon, in 1889, and graduated from the medical school of Willamette University, later the medical school of the University of Oregon, in 1912. Practicing a few years in Salem, he joined the navy at the outset of the U.S. entrance into World War I, and subsequently undertook postgraduate training at several civilian medical schools.

One should add that the rise to the navy's highest medical post, appointment as surgeon general in 1938, which brought the wartime rank of vice admiral and supervision of 175,000 doctors, nurses, and other professionals, fifty-two hospitals, and 278 mobile units, had come in fair part through McIntire's sponsorship by the personal physician of President Woodrow Wilson, Rear Adm. Cary T. Grayson. McIntire's sponsor, a short, slight officer, had graduated from the College of William and Mary and from the medical school of the University of the South in the first years of the present century; it was one of those small schools that the Flexner Report of 1910 eliminated, to the benefit of the medical profession and the latter's patients.[7] The school's curriculum comprised a year of classes. Receiving his degree, young Grayson joined the navy and was assigned to the presidential yacht, the *Mayflower*, a sizable ship even if it sailed mainly the Potomac. He ministered to the crew of well over three hundred sailors and officers during the Theodore Roosevelt and William H. Taft administrations. By chance on duty at the White House during the inauguration of Wilson in 1913, he stitched a cut on the forehead of the new president's sister, who had come for the occasion and fallen during the inaugural luncheon, and thus came to Wilson's attention. Both men were from Virginia, Grayson from a locality so small that Wilson later joked that when a train was passing and happened to stop, a single freight car blocked out the entire village. The two men soon became close friends. In 1915, after Wilson's first wife died of Bright's disease, Grayson introduced him to a beautiful, tall (five feet ten) Washington widow, Edith Bolling Galt, who became the second Mrs. Wilson. About this time the president raised Grayson, a lieutenant commander, to the rank of rear admiral, despite the talk of doubting senators that the new rank meant that the physician would be admiral of the *Boudoir* (they invented the name, to be sure).

Suffice to say of Grayson that after service during and after the war, especially during the time after Wilson suffered a stroke in October 1919, he carried considerable authority, as it was his decision that for a while prevented knowledge of the stroke from getting out and, when it did early in 1920, made possible Wilson's clinging to the presidency even though the ailing chief executive possessed a concentration time of ten minutes and his physical health was irreparably declining. The Navy Department kept Grayson on in the U.S. Naval Dispensary in the early 1920s, so he could minister to Wilson in retirement, and it was in 1925 that the young McIntire had "the privilege of association" with the admiral in Washington, serving in the dispensary.[8]

During the 1920s, the era of Republican presidents, a succession of physicians served the White House, and the assistant White House physician beginning in 1922, Lt. Comdr. Joel T. Boone, who was related to the Kentucky frontiersman, who was short like Grayson and possessed of a carefully trimmed mustache unlike Grayson, and who like the admiral started on the *Mayflower*, became President Herbert Hoover's personal physician in 1929, receiving the temporary rank of captain. When the Roosevelt administration came in on March 4, 1933, Boone hoped to stay, as he had known FDR when the latter was assistant secretary of the navy. Admiral Grayson intervened in favor of McIntire, who received the coveted White House assignment.

In his book Admiral McIntire was frank to say that his appointment came because of friendship with Grayson, and also because the new president required the services of someone who could treat his sinuses, which were sensitive. McIntire was an eye, ear, nose, and throat specialist. He told Grayson that the president was a victim of infantile paralysis. "Cary" only laughed and explained, "The President is as strong as a horse with the exception of a chronic sinus condition that makes him susceptible to colds. That's where you come in." In explaining his own appointment McIntire added that it was a good idea to appoint a member of the armed services, for "being subject to the iron discipline of the armed services, they can be counted on to keep a close mouth about what they say and hear."[9]

The two qualifications of McIntire for the office of presidential physician were awkward recommendations, as would become apparent. He was a protégé of an individual whose medical knowledge had not been celebrated. Boone, who had reason not to like Grayson, remembered that whenever he, Boone, went into Grayson's office at the dispensary, the admiral's desk was covered with unopened medical journals. The medical historian Dr. Bert E. Park has insinuated that one incompetent physician recommended another.[10] As for McIntire's possessing the ability to keep quiet, it raised the possibility that a navy man might not be able to stand against—act independently of, short of resignation—the commander in chief of the nation's armed forces. The higher in rank the personal physician went, doubtless the more constrained that individual's independence.

McIntire undertook his duty with the president, in which he was the physician but his patient was commander in chief, with considerable circumspection. "The health of the chief executive," he wrote, " . . . is his own private business." Perhaps for that reason, also because he was dealing with the president, he made himself inconspicuous in treating Roosevelt. He was accustomed to park his car before the White House each morning, at half past eight or thereabouts, and go to the president's bedroom on the mansion's second floor "for a look-see." He produced neither thermometer nor stethoscope, nor looked at the presidential tongue nor felt of the pulse, and rarely asked a question. He sat while the president ate breakfast or looked at the morning papers, which it was FDR's custom to do while lounging in bed. This procedure "told all I wanted to know." By this he meant the presidential color, tone of voice, tilt of the chin, "the way he tackled his orange juice, cereal, and eggs." Satisfied on such points the admiral went off to his other duties, which during the war were many, an enormous number of administrative tasks. But in afternoons he was back outside the executive offices, promptly at half past five, for another look-see, checking what work the president had left in his "in" box that might become the evening's work, checking also that Roosevelt went for a swim in the pool or had a before-dinner rest.[11] When the president's physician accompanied the president on trips he usually gave FDR the "once over" at bedtime.

This was the routine, and when the president increased his workload the presidential physician had to accommodate himself to what the president insisted upon as needing to be done. On some occasions all McIntire could do was "to save as much as possible out of the wreck and watch for danger signs." Roosevelt suffered another apparent attack of influenza in 1941. The muscular structure deteriorated because of lack of exercise, which McIntire had to cut down on as a means of conserving Roosevelt's strength. The kidneys and liver nonetheless functioned normally, the blood picture was all right, "and cardiovascular measurements stayed on a good level."[12]

Because everything essentially was all right, the admiral related, he made suitable explanations to the newspaper press. When the president ran for an unprecedented fourth term, could FDR stand the strain of another four years? McIntire first asked his consultants, who returned an affirmative answer. Privately he told the president to be careful, for with care "I gave it as my best judgment that his chances of winning through to 1948 were *good*." Any indisposition soon disappeared because the president possessed the stamina to resist an attack of grippe, a sinus flare-up, or absorption of infection from a tooth. "His blood pressure remained on an excellent level . . . and his cardiovascular measurements were within normal standards for a man of his age." After the Teheran Conference of November–December 1943, the president was tired, but all was well physically, despite a journey that covered 17,742 sea, land, and air miles, with stops in Cairo, Malta, and Sicily. Roosevelt was tired, for the year had been an exhausting one, but was not in straits. The correspondents agreed that upon return he looked "in the pink."[13]

Admiral McIntire always was careful with his press statements, and said early in 1944 that the president was "in his best health ever." March 6 of that year it was "the finest possible health" and "in perfect shape." June 8 the president's health was "excellent in all respects." Roosevelt's correspondence secretary, William D. Hassett, was delighted to hear the last appraisal, and wrote in his diary that day that "the Boss" was going serenely on while his enemies railed about his being a tired old man. (Composer of letters that the president signed but were not important enough for the president to write, an avuncular, dignified New Englander known within the executive offices as "the Bishop," Hassett was to watch FDR carefully in coming months.) For the fourth inaugural, January 20, 1945, McIntire allowed as to how "everything's fine," the president carrying a "thunder of a lot of work and getting away with it." Generally speaking, he wrote after the president passed on, he had not drawn FDR in "glowing" statements but in cautious judgment, with the conclusion that he was in "excellent condition for a man of his age" (in January 1945 the president celebrated his sixty-third birthday). In 1946, McIntire allowed inclusion in his book of a statement in italics about the "man of his age" remark: *I stand by that judgment today without amendment or apology.*[14]

When the patient suddenly died in Warm Springs, where Roosevelt was being watched over by an assistant physician, not the admiral, who was in Washington, that saddening Thursday afternoon, April 12, 1945, McIntire found himself making an explanation or two. The secretary of state, Edward R. Stettinius Jr., who had replaced Cordell Hull in November 1944, talked with McIntire, who said that "this was a complete shock to him—it was something absolutely new and came as a complete surprise. The president's blood pressure was all right and had been for some time, and there was absolutely no apparent cause for the stroke." Amb. Joseph E. Davies hurried over to the White House and saw McIntire who said the trouble was that Roosevelt, who had been losing weight, dropping from 190 pounds to 160, had lost it too fast. FDR had been trying to put it back on, but "others," McIntire told Davies, prevailed upon him to continue to diet. Some months later Secy. of the Interior Harold L. Ickes heard the admiral explain that "the President's heart had given away under the great pressure of the load that he was carrying. He told me that no one could predict that the President would go out the way that he did."[15]

At the end of 1945 and into 1946 when McIntire was writing his book, with the assistance of the professional writer George Creel, it may have been the admiral's confusion on and after April 12, 1945, that led the two men, McIntire and Creel, to an uneasy relationship. McIntire needed to make some sort of public statement, beyond his recent press remarks and his momentary comments to Stettinius, Davies, and Ickes. But the book was not easy to produce. Having engaged Creel, the admiral was wary about telling him anything. He virtually refused to go beyond his public statements. In a memorandum for Creel that he dictated he said that in 1944

> A very thorough physical examination was conducted in the last week of March and a diagnosis was made of acute bronchitis. There was no evidence found of any other organic defect, although his blood pressure was noted to vary quite considerably from day to day and to be elevated over his normal range. Although the heart continued to carry its load satisfactorily it was realized that there was definite danger of complications arising unless his respiratory infections were cleared.[16]

Relations between author and collaborator nearly snapped. At one juncture Creel, whose intent face supported any assumption that he was an intent, hard-nosed journalist, wrote and asked for information "For God's sake." He added, "do not fall down," and mentioned two letters he wished McIntire to obtain, testifying to the president's last days and hours.[17] The book came out on time, within the year as planned, and was almost absurdly thin. Alert readers could have had the impression that Creel created nearly all of it.

The problems with the book may have had less to do with McIntire's confusion over what to say than Creel's desire to publish, so as to obtain payment for his services, coupled with his tendency to embellish and overexplain, which had brought an aura of untrustworthiness to his career as a writer.[18] McIntire's virtual coauthor—

the title page showed Creel's name in type the same size as that of McIntire—had enjoyed a long literary career that began during the muckraking era at the turn of the century, down to the opening of the world war in Europe, when Creel and other writers exposed the evils of American society and politics, especially the "shame of the cities." The muckrakers were a varied group, some trustworthy, others not. Ida M. Tarbell, who wrote about the Standard Oil Company, was an admirable writer who thirty years later published *The Nationalizing of Business: 1878–1898,* in the series "A History of American Life," which was an ornament to professional historical writing in the 1920s, 1930s, and 1940s. Others of the muckrakers were not so trustworthy, for Samuel Hopkins Adams had written well about patent medicines and followed in the 1920s with an absurd novel about a president of the United States, a thinly veiled account of Teapot Dome and President Warren G. Harding, and followed that novel with an equally absurd nonfictional account of the Harding era. Lincoln Steffens, author of city exposés, went to the Soviet Union and believed everything he saw ("I have seen the future and it works"). In 1905 Upton Sinclair produced an unbelievable account of abuse in the meatpacking industry in Chicago, *The Jungle,* with a story about a man shoveling dead rats into sausage and of another man who could not shovel rats because he was making up a vat of lard and fell into it and was sold as lard.

In Creel's case his early journalism may have been all right but some of his services to himself distinctly were not. With the blessing of Secy. of the Navy Josephus Daniels in 1917—Daniels had been publisher of the *Raleigh (N.C.) News and Observer*—Creel became chairman of the wartime Committee on Public Information that supervised dozens of writers, including many American historians, who turned out propaganda about the war, including slanted accounts of German public and private behavior. After this service he allowed himself to be employed by an anonymous individual to approach his wartime sponsor, Secretary Daniels, over permitting the U.S. Navy's oil reserves at Teapot Dome, Wyoming, and Elk Hills, California, to be leased by private oilmen. Daniels refused the suggestion, for which Creel was paid five thousand dollars. Four years later, early in 1924, the oilman Edward L. Doheny avowed that he had paid Creel. The writer said he had not known that, but made no effort to repay the money, as perhaps he should have, although such an effort would not have covered his willingness to take pay for influencing a public figure who happened to be his sponsor.

In viewing the book there is yet another point that needs discussion, which is whether the admiral, so busy with his many duties other than watching over the health (or illness) of the president, did not have time in 1945–1946 to calculate what he should say about Roosevelt, how he, a physician, should explain himself. During the war he could have believed that the need to keep a closed mouth, as remarked in his book, required him to prevaricate about the president's illness in the name of national security. He then might have acquired his literary collaborator, Creel, almost before he could convince himself of what to say, for the end of the Pacific war did not come until August 14 and there were the immediate problems of bringing the soldiers back from East Asia and of demobilizing large portions of the navy. He might have gotten himself into the collaboration before he realized what was going on, and found himself embarrassed by Creel's pushing him for material and hence allowed the freelancer to write it up. Before McIntire could have faced up to the book project he might have seen the end product ready, jacketed and priced and in the bookstores. Thereupon he could have decided to face the music by repeating what he had said during the war about his commander in chief.

The peculiarity of McIntire's position that Roosevelt was in the best of health for a man of his age is that the admiral for the rest of his life maintained it; he died of a heart attack in 1959 in Chicago where he was general secretary of the International College of Physicians and Surgeons. He could have said no more, refused to be interviewed. Instead he became belligerent in reaction to any claim that he might have been wrong about his patient. On March 5, 1951, James A. Farley, the former chairman of the Democratic National Committee, published a letter to the editor of the *New York Times* in which he quoted an entry in his diary of July 26, 1944, at the time of the party's convention in Chicago that renominated Roosevelt. Farley had broken with FDR in 1940 and was unforgiving of what he considered the president's perfidy in encouraging presidential candidates for the 1940 election and then taking the nomination himself, and he could have published the letter to the *Times* for that reason, another nail in the coffin of Roosevelt's reputation. One must presume he wrote only to make his point: "Anyone with a grain of common sense would surely realize from the appearance of the President that he is not a well man and that there is not a chance in the world for him to carry on for four years more and face the problems that a president will have before him; he just can't survive another presidential term." The Farley letter galvanized McIntire to a defense of his position about Roosevelt's health. The day after the letter appeared in the *Times* the *Washington Star* published a lead editorial quoting Farley. It led McIntire to a three-column response in the *Star* four days later, repeating what he had said in his book. He followed with an article in *U.S. News and World Report* for March 23, in the form of questions and answers, under the title "Did U.S. Elect a Dying President?" All the way through the outraged admiral stood his ground, repeating what he had said about Roosevelt's physical problems during the war and in the subsequently published book. To the question with which *U.S. News*'s editors began the article, a question that by then any informed reader would have answered with a resounding "Yes!" he countered with a resounding "No!"

There was one more aspect of McIntire's conduct that never has been explained, an aspect that seems almost understandable yet one is unsure. This is the disappearance of President Roosevelt's hospital chart, kept at the U.S. Navy's general hospital at Bethesda, Maryland, in which Admiral McIntire had written from 1933 onward, and in which his diagnoses and treatments of Roosevelt's illnesses could be traced, were it possible to see the chart. It has defied the most detailed efforts to discover it. Historians have searched the massive National Personnel Records Center in St. Louis where records of all federal employees, military and civil, are stored. They have asked for examination of the VIP files at the center, and officials have searched the pseudonyms under which Roosevelt's medical tests at Bethesda were made. Nothing has availed. The chart was a large one, two inches thick, and would have proved a highly interesting document. Seemingly it was destroyed. Admiral McIntire kept it in the Bethesda safe, and only he, the hospital's commanding officer, and the executive officer possessed the keys or combination, whatever was necessary to open the safe.

2

The cancer theory, in its contention that President Roosevelt died of stomach cancer or from a melanoma, amounted in both of its assertions to nought but theory. There were appearances that raised the possibility of cancer. Nothing has emerged to certify that what several physicians have asserted as likelihood was anything more.

What inspired the rumor that Roosevelt's physical decline in 1944–1945 derived from stomach cancer was the acutely painful stomach cramps the president suffered on the night of November 28, 1943, when in the capital of Iran at the Teheran Conference. The attack began at dinner. According to one of the people present, "Roosevelt was about to say something . . . when suddenly, in the flick of an eye, he turned green and great drops of sweat began to bead off his face; he put a shaky hand to his forehead."[19] The attack caught everyone by surprise, for the president had made no complaint and there had been no sign of discomfort. The president's assistant, Harry Hopkins, had him wheeled to his room, where Admiral McIntire made a quick examination. Hopkins returned and to everyone's relief reported nothing more than a mild attack of indigestion. Because this was the Middle East, and FDR was staying in the compound of the Soviet embassy (Stalin had advised that he move there because of security reasons), the attack first was attributed by the whisperers, the workers in the rumor factories, to nothing less than poisoning: the president was being poisoned. After that rumor subsided, for the Soviets surely would not have been that direct in their hospitality, it seemed more natural, more likely, to define the attack as a sign of stomach cancer.

Supporting the possibility of stomach cancer was the presidential indisposition after Roosevelt returned from Teheran. He was not feeling well. He constantly was tired. Something indefinable was ailing him. As was his wont, he repaired, sometimes week after week, to Hyde Park. His train would be readied in the basement of the Bureau of Engraving and Printing Annex and would leave on a Thursday evening, shortly before midnight (so, it was said, his staff, which meant two secretaries and secret servicemen and telegraphic and telephone people, could all draw an extra day's per diem; an alternative explanation was that, being superstitious, the president did not want to leave on a Friday). Arriving in Highland, New York, the station across the Hudson from Poughkeepsie and nearest to the president's estate in Hyde Park, the train would stand on a siding until the following Monday night, and retrace its route down to the capital.

The trips to Hyde Park and back, fortunately, must have been fairly easy, despite the distance. The president did not like to travel more than fifty miles per hour on a train because of the rocking, although overnight trips allowed faster speeds. The president's train consisted of a communications car, a baggage car, compartment–drawing room sleepers, and a dining car. The last car of "POTUS," code word for the train of the president of the United States, was the Ferdinand Magellan, specially armored, with three-inch-thick window glass, weighing 285,000 pounds, almost twice the weight of an ordinary Pullman. It possessed a lounge, four bedrooms including a master bedroom for the president that was equipped with a shower, together with a dining room and kitchen.

Yet all the effort to give the president enlarged weekends in the near pastoral environment he loved so well failed to revive him. Part of the problem was that upon arrival back in Washington he would find that work had piled up, not merely paperwork but the business of seeing people who, once they entered the presidential office, always sought to stay longer than the ten or fifteen minutes assigned them. The routine of that winter of 1943–1944 hence always seemed to stretch out, the long weekends at Hyde Park made little difference, failed to refresh. It did seem that something was gnawing at the president's vitals, an ailment that rest and relaxation could not resolve. That, so the rumor factories announced, was quite possibly cancer, and because of the upset that had occurred at Teheran it probably was stomach cancer.

In March and again in May 1944, Roosevelt was seen by an honorary medical consultant of the navy, the well-known Boston surgeon Dr. Frank H. Lahey, founder of the Lahey Clinic, and word of these consultations must have gotten out. Why would a surgeon be seeing the president, unless he was planning to or in fact did cut something out? In the years after Roosevelt's death Dr. Lahey himself contributed to the possibility of stomach cancer, for on at least one occasion, visiting friends at a club in New Hampshire, he told a small group that he had seen the president at the White House and examined him and found an appalling situation. After the examination, according to Lahey's story, he and the president held a conference. The president smiled his most engaging smile and inquired, "You have good news for me, Dr. Lahey?"

"Mr. President," was the response, "you may not care for what I have to say."

"That will be all, Dr. Lahey," said President Roosevelt.[20]

Lahey lived until 1953, and sometime after the two consultations with the president the surgeon, who was a prolific writer, wrote a memorandum setting out his White House experiences. Shortly before his death he entrusted the memorandum to his longtime friend and business manager of the clinic, Linda M. Strand. Therein lies something of a tale, involving not merely Mrs. Strand, who was executor of Lahey's estate, but Dr. Harry Goldsmith, who in the years after President Roosevelt's death was a surgical resident at Memorial–Sloan Kettering Cancer Center in New York City, thereafter surgical professor at the Dartmouth Medical School. More recently, in the 1980s and 1990s, Dr. Goldsmith has taken interest in Alzheimer's disease and has traveled widely, not merely in the United States but in Europe, attending and treating patients.

Dr. Goldsmith in 1963, while in his residency in New York, heard the cancer surgeon Dr. George T. Pack say in a lecture that Dr. Lahey told him about Roosevelt's stomach cancer, and this was the beginning of Goldsmith's search for the truth about what ailed the wartime president in 1944–1945.[21] According to Lahey, who told Pack, the president suffered from a malignant tumor, and Lahey had advised the president not to run for a fourth term. At the time of the lecture Pack told Goldsmith that he, Pack, possessed notebooks in which he had written down what Lahey told him and that when time permitted he would make these notebooks available to Goldsmith. Not long thereafter Pack died. Goldsmith applied to the executor of Pack's estate, and received access to the notebooks, only to discover that there was only a book and a half and that they did not touch on the conversation with Lahey.[22]

Curiosity piqued by Pack's lecture and his own inability to discover the notes, Goldsmith years later became aware of the existence of the Lahey memorandum in the possession of Mrs. Strand. After a complicated effort to find the former business manager of the Lahey Clinic and executor of the Lahey estate, Dr. Goldsmith eventually found her in retirement in Florida. Mrs. Strand proved a reticent woman, not easy to approach, but gradually Dr. Goldsmith won her confidence.

What happened in regard to the Lahey memorandum, a series of happenings actually, is worth describing, as it displays the way in which important historical documents sometimes become available. Lahey had advised his executor that she should publish the memorandum if for any reason his handling of the Roosevelt case should come into question. Dr. Goldsmith convinced Mrs. Strand that the issue of Roosevelt's death indeed was in question and it was time to publish. The memo was in the hands of lawyers for the Lahey estate, and they refused to give it up. Goldsmith went to court in 1985 and in the name of Mrs. Strand sued for return of the memo.

In passing it is necessary to guess at the reason the Lahey lawyers refused to release the memo, which may well have been their doubts about the probity of Linda Strand. As business manager of the clinic she had been a formidable figure. The clinic's founder had established his hospital in belief that patients should pay according to their ability, which meant a wide variation in the size of bills. Mrs. Strand made up the bills. In Lahey's last years there was a good deal of dissension among the clinic's staff physicians, part of it feeling against Mrs. Strand. She had arranged that all dictation at the clinic should be done by a pool, and placed her own people in the pool. She put relatives on the payroll. At one point after Lahey's death she installed herself as director of the clinic, until removed— because she was not a physician—by the trustees. Within weeks of the end of his life Dr. Lahey gave Mrs. Strand a lifetime contract in the amount of fifty thousand dollars a year, at that time a very large income. Lahey had been drawn into an argument with his successor as director, Dr. Richard B. Cattell, and believed he was protecting Mrs. Strand. The trustees sought to settle this awkward situation and in 1962 awarded Mrs. Strand a lifetime income that with other payments cost more than a half million dollars.

How much of the controversy over Mrs. Strand was known to the judge of the county court to whom Dr. Goldsmith went for release of the memorandum is difficult to say, but the judge refused to release the memo, ruling that a situation had not yet arisen to bring Dr. Lahey's handling of the Roosevelt case into question.

Meanwhile, Mrs. Strand, who in 1985 was eighty-nine years old, entered the case in substitution for Dr. Goldsmith. The Lahey Clinic entered the suit against Mrs. Strand, for it did not want the memorandum published because, its lawyers said, it would affect the doctor-patient relationship. The suit, denied in county court, went to the Massachusetts Supreme Court, which decided that Mrs. Strand should have the memo. She died in 1988, and in 1990 Dr. Goldsmith called the Lahey Clinic and said he had a copy of the memo and would release it in good time, presumably when he published the book-length manuscript he was writing concerning his relations with Mrs. Strand and his long effort to advance the diagnosis of Dr. Lahey that President Roosevelt died from stomach cancer.

But while Dr. Goldsmith was clearing the way for publication of the Lahey memorandum, he advanced another theory for the death of President Roosevelt. It was another cancer theory, namely, that the president died of a malignant melanoma, that is, the lesion visible over his left eyebrow. It was an ingenious possibility. In his article in a medical journal published in 1979 titled "Unanswered Mysteries in the Death of Franklin D. Roosevelt," in which he set out his account of Dr. Pack's lecture, Dr. Goldsmith published a succession of photographs of the president beginning with the year 1932. Each of them showed the lesion, and as the years passed the lesion grew, with fingers that began to reach down into the president's eyebrow. Then in the photograph for 1944, the lesion disappeared. The disappearance raised the possibility that the lesion had been a melanoma that could have spread into the president's gastrointestinal tract. The disappearance cast doubt over a statement by Admiral McIntire that the president had never had any operation other than removal of a wen, a sebaceous cyst, from the back of his head, and extraction of a wisdom tooth.

A University of Kansas medical historian, Dr. Robert P. Hudson, professor of history and medicine at his university's medical school, gave an address in 1986 at a conference of the American Association for the History of Medicine, of which he was president, in which he said that the sudden brain hemorrhage that killed the president was attributable either to a malignant brain tumor or to severe cardiovascular disease, "both of which, in my opinion, he suffered." The address, at Rochester, New York, was widely reported by the Associated Press. Hudson told delegates to his association meeting that Roosevelt suffered from a malignant melanoma and that it might have spread to his brain by 1944, the year he ran for a fourth term. Diagnosis of the cancer, Hudson said, probably came in the spring of 1944, yet the president's personal physician "repeatedly deceived the public" by denying Roosevelt's illness.[23]

In actual fact the theory of a melanoma had a history that reached back considerably before appearance of the Goldsmith article and the address by Dr. Hudson. Its first reference in the literature was probably an article in a periodical by the name of *Modern Medicine* published in 1961 by Dr. F. M. Massie. This physician was recounting a medical meeting in St. Louis in 1949, at which a surgeon from George Washington University School of Medicine and from Walter Reed General Hospital in Washington presented a paper on treatment of malignant melanomas and illustrated it with slides and specimens. All of the slides and specimens contained hospital serial numbers save a section of brain with a large metastatic melanoma bearing only a date, April 14, 1945—the day Roosevelt's body arrived in Washington from Warm Springs.

Unfortunately, several awkwardnesses have surrounded this Massie article. For one thing, it appeared in a periodical that is impossible to find; there have been several periodicals named *Modern Medicine*, and the citation for Massie's article if followed to the most likely periodical leads to a page bearing only an advertisement. For another thing, it is impossible to obtain more information from Massie. The present writer discovered another article by him indicating that he was a Kentucky physician, and application to the Kentucky Medical Association revealed that he died in 1985. Too, Massie's account defied the well-known fact that Roosevelt's body was not autopsied, and if it had been there would have been little sense in taking it to Walter Reed, the army's hospital, when the late president's records were all at Bethesda, the navy's hospital. One also must wonder why after hearing a sensational paper Massie waited a dozen years to publish an article about it.

The Massie article appeared in 1961, and there was a further publication by the well-known British medical historian Dr. Hugh

L'Etang, in a book titled *The Pathology of Leadership*, which appeared in England in 1969 and was republished in the United States in 1970 and received considerable attention. In a chapter on President Roosevelt's illness and death L'Etang repeated Massie's allegations.[24]

There were, then, despite the unavailability of the Lahey memorandum and the awkwardnesses of the Massie-L'Etang-Goldsmith-Hudson contentions about a malignant melanoma, these two theories of the president's death by cancer. The two could be interpreted as one, in that the stomach cancer mentioned in the Lahey memorandum could have been caused by a melanoma that metastasized to the gastrointestinal tract.

Is there any possible way to dismiss the cancer theories? The theory about stomach cancer will not disappear until Dr. Goldsmith publishes the Lahey memorandum. Yet there is testimony by Admiral McIntire's assistant, Dr. Howard G. Bruenn, about whom much more will be said later, that when he was attending the president during a vacation in South Carolina in April–May 1944, Roosevelt suffered two more attacks similar to the one at Teheran and that they were gallbladder attacks. After return from the Teheran Conference the president felt ill, was sliding downhill, and Dr. McIntire advised a vacation, which lasted nearly a month. The vacation was spent at the estate of the financier Bernard M. Baruch, a quiet, restful place comprising a large house and tens of thousands of acres, sufficiently remote so that it was easy to control access to the nation's chief executive and his party. The president enjoyed himself at the estate, known as Hobcaw, remaining in bed in mornings, as was his wont, and otherwise amusing himself with fishing and reception of a few visitors. Evenings went in a round of cocktails and dinner and everyone to bed according to doctor's orders. The only illnesses of the president at Hobcaw were the two gallbladder attacks, as Bruenn diagnosed them.

The first of the attacks at Hobcaw occurred on April 28, when the president felt severe abdominal pains, which Bruenn treated with a .5 grain of codeine administered by hypodermic injection. The distress subsided by May 1. Next day came another attack, which lasted forty-eight hours. The president was acutely uncomfortable, and Bruenn treated him with heat to the abdomen and codeine again administered hypodermically.

When the president returned to Washington it was arranged that he would have X rays taken of his gallbladder on May 26. One of the president's cousins was staying with him at the White House at this time, Margaret, or Daisy, Suckley, who was slight of build, plain-faced, and retiring. Daisy lived in a Victorian mansion in Rhinebeck, ten miles to the north of Hyde Park, and saw a great deal of FDR. According to her diary she and the president's daughter, Anna, visiting in the White House, helped him take the dye pills at five-minute intervals that produced the color needed for the gallbladder test and accompanied him to Bethesda for the occasion. The X rays showed a group of cholesterol stones. Bruenn and McIntire accordingly placed him on a low-fat diet of eighteen hundred calories to prevent abdominal symptoms, as well as reduce his weight, which was 188 pounds. Because of atrophy of the president's legs and thighs, his weight had concentrated in the chest and abdomen. One should add that the weight loss induced by the diet later seemed to support the stomach cancer theory.

Years later when Dr. Goldsmith published his article he asked therein why Bruenn, who was not a surgeon, had not sought out Dr. Lahey to examine the president after the gallbladder attacks. Dr. McIntire in his book related that Lahey and another honorary medical consultant of the navy, the Atlanta internist Dr. James E. Paullin, president of the American Medical Association (AMA), gave the president "another going-over" at this time and found nothing seriously wrong, and recommended only avoidance of overwork, with a rest period after luncheon and relaxation in evenings. Dr. Bruenn published an article on Roosevelt's illness in 1970 and said he was so certain the Hobcaw upsets were gallbladder attacks that he felt entirely easy about treating them himself.[25]

As for the possibility of a melanoma, the record similarly reveals nothing extraordinary, although it contains a small obscurity. In February 1944 the president went to Bethesda for removal of a sebaceous cyst of some size that was at the back of his neck or perhaps the back of his head. It is not certain whether the surgeon who did this work, a physician from the Mayo Clinic, Dr. Winchell M. Craig, chief of surgery at Bethesda, took off the nevus over the president's eyebrow at this time. Bruenn, who began to see the president late in March, could only have heard of the operation on the cyst or cysts. To one interviewer many years later he said there was removal of a single cyst. To another he said that Craig (whom he erroneously described as Dr. Winchell) took off both.[26] Because as Dr. Goldsmith observed from the photographs, the cyst over the left eyebrow disappeared at just about this time, one must assume that Craig removed both of them.

Daisy Suckley's diary offers a remarkable setting out of the president's problems with illness, and her description of removal of the cyst from the neck or head was full and explicit. On February 1, Daisy wrote, when she was staying in the Yellow Room, as she described it, on the third floor of the White House, after dinner that evening, about half past eight, the president sent for her, and she discovered him with Anna and her husband, John Boettiger, a newspaperman. The company talked about the forthcoming removal of the wen at Bethesda, including who should go with the president for the occasion. Afterward, the Boettigers said good night, Daisy left, "& the P. tackled a pile of dispatches etc."[27] For the operation next day Daisy and Anna went along, and when the presidential car arrived outside Bethesda they could see heads in every window of the hospital, for the coming of the president had been advertised and everyone knew of the visit. When the president passed through the lobby of the hospital in his wheelchair, onlookers surrounded him. He went up to see his ill assistant, Hopkins, and then passed on to the operating room. Dr. McIntire and three other doctors were there, including of course Craig, and McIntire asked Daisy and Anna if they would like to come in and watch. Daisy had the impression that the admiral did not really want them, and they demurred. In forty-five minutes or so it was over, and the president came out in a good mood, having undergone a local anesthetic, and wore only a patch bandage on his head. Dr. McIntire said the wen was like a small egg, and came out without the slightest trouble.

On February 4 the president told his press conference about the wen because, Daisy wrote that day, he did not want huge headlines: "The President Under the Knife . . ." He said he had had the wen for twenty years. Someone at the hospital telephoned the press that he spent an hour in the hospital and emerged with a dressing on his head. Three reporters, according to Daisy who would have heard the story from the president who might have exaggerated, called up the president's press secretary, Stephen T. Early, in the middle of the night and asked what was going on.[28]

Roosevelt wrote his longtime friend, the political boss of the Bronx, Edward J. Flynn, on February 8, and informed Flynn of what he had undergone. "My head is coming along," he wrote, "—they took out eight stitches on Sunday and I hope you will enjoy that horrible process as much as I did!"[29] By "enjoy" he must have meant "enjoy the telling," not wishing such an occasion upon Boss Flynn.

There were some small aftereffects. Daisy returned to her home and on Friday, February 11, wrote, "The P. just called up. Has had a heavy week & still has a constant headache—The bandage is off his head & Admiral McIntire brushed the hair over it & pronounced it 'beautiful!' " When the president came up to Hyde Park on Wednesday, February 23, he arrived at nine o'clock in the morning and came over to the library shortly afterward, where Daisy was helping rearrange the presidential papers. (The Franklin D. Roosevelt Library, a handsome stone edifice constructed with private funds, had been dedicated in 1941.) "The back of the head is almost healed up," she reported, "& won't show at all, when the scab is off & the hair has grown. He looks well, but is tired as usual . . ."[30]

Surrounded by physicians as the neck or back-of-the-head cyst came off, and with photographs thereafter showing no above-the-eyebrow cyst, Roosevelt must have had the latter removed, perhaps with the little electric-needle machine that facilitated such removals in those times. It would seem incredible that Dr. Craig, who after the war returned to the Mayo Clinic as head of the Department of Neurosurgery, would have failed to see the eyebrow cyst that might have been a melanoma and done nothing about it. Or, removing it, failed to have a slide made and analyzed. The president may not always have had the best of medical care but surely at least one of the four physicians in the Bethesda operating room on February 2, 1944, would have noticed the wen on the president's eyebrow and inquired about it.

*T*he turning point in President Roosevelt's diagnosis, in discovering what ailed him, why his energy level was down, came on March 28, 1944, when a new physician, a cardiologist, was brought into the case. This was the young naval lieutenant commander Dr. Bruenn, who was mentioned in connection with the gallbladder attacks. Until Bruenn's appearance the president was feeling up and down; McIntire was getting nowhere. The admiral's procedure of parking his car and joining the president each morning at breakfast time, and watching the verve with which Roosevelt ate his breakfast, was little short of ludicrous. It was no better than the old-time analysis of a country doctor, perhaps the physician in the well-known picture of the devoted man of medicine sitting at the bedside of a sufferer, doing his best. Nor were the explanations of cancer, of either stomach cancer or melanoma, any better; they were as far removed from the real trouble as were McIntire's ruminations about influenza and bronchitis. The trouble was advanced cardiovascular disease, and it was Bruenn who not merely diagnosed it but insisted upon his diagnosis in such a way that he forced remedial action—that is, such as could be taken at the time, given the treatment that obtained in 1944–1945.

1

When the president came back from the Teheran Conference early in December 1943, he did not feel well, and what stirred concern about his condition and eventually aroused his daughter, Anna, to insist upon a consultation, which meant a general physical examination, was the inability of the president to "come out of" his lassitude, his difficulty with keeping going.

There were few signs beforehand. The president's special counsel, his speechwriter, Samuel I. Rosenman, was so close to the president that most of the time he did not notice anything. Known as Judge Rosenman for having served on the New York State Supreme Court, a longtime Roosevelt intimate, short of stature, cherubic of mien, and shrewd, he missed little but did not observe FDR's failing health. Daisy Suckley who saw her cousin when he came home, which was often, or herself was invited down to the White House, admired FDR so much that she may have overdrawn an episode that happened shortly before Teheran. When the president called up from Washington on October 18 he told her he was not feeling well. This was not untypical, as he poured out to her his physical ills, real or imaginary, or she divined them from him, for she liked him so much she fastened upon anything as possibly dangerous and thereby made him feel worse. He told Daisy he had fallen asleep twice while trying to write a message to Congress. He may have been saying waggishly that his auditors would be so boring that the very thought of talking to them drove him to somnolence. People who saw him less could observe more. In May 1943, so Prime Minister Winston Churchill's personal physician, Charles Wilson, Lord Moran, who seemed more prescient than he was, later related, Churchill discerned a downturn. "Have you noticed that the President is a very tired man?" Moran's patient asked. "His mind seems closed; he seems to have lost his wonderful elasticity." The comment might have come because Roosevelt had miffed Churchill in some manner and the prime minister interpreted it as illness. Moran attributed the comment to the prime minister's clairvoyance: "I could not follow all that was in the P.M.'s mind . . ." Nothing might have been in the P.M.'s mind; or Moran, who liked to come in to see the prime minister after breakfast and annoy him with questions, might have received an answer with the purpose of turning the conversation and getting the physician on his way.[1]

The day after the president telephoned Daisy he called again, when his cousin was at the library. "I thought you might read in the paper that I am sick and I had better tell you, first," he said, almost worrying her to death. He evidently, Daisy thought, was suffering from the grippe, ached all over, and had a fever up to 104¼. A professional self-medicator, she decided at once that he caught such things from visitors when he was susceptible under stress; he himself had explained once that he caught everything in sight, all his life had been that way. His cousin decided that rest in bed would do him good. "It is so thoughtful of him to call up—I hope he'll let me know how he is, tonight." Fortunately he called her up again, his fever almost down to normal, head still heavy. He sounded cheerful and said, perhaps the reason for cheer, that he would come up to Hyde Park on Thursday evening and return to Washington the following Tuesday evening, the five-day vacation maybe would help for the long trip to come ten days thereafter.[2]

Daisy drew out her cousin's aches and ills, and noted in her diary for October 29 that he still ached and felt tired. She had found him on the sofa in his Hyde Park study, sorting magazines, and begged him to go to bed early, "a useless begging, as he goes when he feels like it!" Next day, October 30, what she described as influenza had left him "rather miserable, and very tired." As was his custom "he can't give in to it." At noon he was terribly sleepy and let her take him to the large chair by the fireplace and put his feet on a two-step stool. She went out to get ready for lunch, and he fell sound asleep.[3]

Daisy saw the president again before he left on the trip, and on November 5, Friday, found him "very tired" after a long day, but keyed up, unable to relax. She noted that he had started taking coffee for breakfast, evidently a momentous change. He did that because on the long trip there would not be anything else to drink. It was obviously not good for him, she wrote, for it showed in his hands, which became a little shaky. She told her diary interestingly that he worried a bit because of swelling in his ankles "which comes when he is tired." She was comforted that the president's physical therapist, Lt. Comdr. George A. Fox, whose presence in the White House had commenced during the Wilson administration and after a break until the Coolidge administration had become permanent, resolved the ankle swelling by rubbing the presidential ankles before dinner. Fox, whose training Daisy considered thorough, employed an electric vibrator with the ankles at bedtime. This helped the circulation. Daisy believed that her cousin needed a slow massage all over his feet and legs at least twenty minutes each day.[4]

So it went prior to Teheran, and the cause of Roosevelt's not feeling well now and then could have been nought but too much activity, too many people applying for his limited time in the executive offices. Churchill's comment to Moran was the first one in the physician's voluminous accountings of everything around him, and no more appeared for many pages. Whatever evidences of illness were present before Teheran, they were difficult to be sure of.

After return there was a change. The president, it was first said, suffered from what Daisy defined as grippe and others including McIntire as influenza, and then it was postflu. At Christmastime he felt like a "boiled owl." Early in January the director of the budget, Harold D. Smith, saw him in his bedroom, and he was no better. Smith had not seen him since Teheran, and said he was sorry to learn of the illness. "He commented that the damn Washington weather had gotten him down, but that he thought he probably did not have any active bugs which I would catch. He seemed annoyed that after successfully completing his trip he should be laid low by the flu." Smith said everyone around Washington had been afflicted with similar difficulty, and he agreed. But the president did not give the budget message, an important matter, the attention he had given it on previous occasions. "He seemed worried and worn out. I have never seen him so listless. He is not his acute usual self. In fact, I was quite startled, at one stage when he was about two-thirds through the Message. As he sat up in bed, I saw his head nod. I could not see his eyes, but it seemed as though they were completely shut. Yet, he said something to the effect that 'this paragraph is good.' . . . I have seen the President before when he was ill in his bedroom, but never so groggy."[5]

A week or so later FDR was still in trouble. On January 8 he called Daisy to say he was coming to Hyde Park "for a week of change & to get back to normal."[6] Evidently Hyde Park failed to work its usual magic, for on January 28 the president told Hassett that he "still has a headache every evening as an aftermath of the flu." It was the first reference in the correspondence secretary's diary to Roosevelt's ill health.[7]

February 6, a Sunday, another of the almost weekly escapes from Washington to Hyde Park, marked the first evening when the headache disappeared. Two days later it was back again. Daisy told herself and probably her cousin that "it must come from being constantly tired—never getting *really* rested, specially since having the flu."[8]

When Daisy observed the headache she added something to her diary that was of special interest, for it showed one reason the undoubtedly weary president was not getting attention beyond the advice of Daisy and the diagnoses of Admiral McIntire, both of which were possibly of equal value, Daisy's kind words if anything of more value. She had suggested to her beloved FDR that he should take a rest or a short drive—every afternoon, Daisy said, for she was nothing if not methodical in doling out her medical advice. Roosevelt said he hated to drive alone. Daisy said he should ask Mrs. Roosevelt. He laughed and said, with the maliciousness of which he sometimes was capable, "I would have to make an appointment a week ahead!"[9]

There, surely, was part of the trouble, because except for Daisy he was getting little sympathy. The truth was that Eleanor Roosevelt was insensitive to her husband's rapidly declining health. When the Roosevelts' daughter, Anna, tall, slim, a most attractive member of the presidential family, confided her concerns, Mrs. Roosevelt dismissed them, saying she was not interested in "physiology." Will and determination were what conquered illness, and her husband, the daughter remembered learning from her mother, was only anxious about the turbulent private life of their son Elliott, who although then in the U.S. Army Air Forces was finishing off a marriage so he could wed the Hollywood actress Faye Emerson.[10]

The marriage of Franklin and Eleanor Roosevelt long since had lapsed, and Daisy at this time—she was to learn more later—did not understand that fact. She knew something about the former Lucy Mercer, married to Winthrop Rutherfurd, whom Eleanor had brought into the Roosevelt household during the Wilson administration as a social secretary; in her diary during the early weeks of 1944 Daisy remarked that one Sunday late in March the president entertained the striking Mrs. Rutherfurd who had come up from New York, took her around the estate, and showed her his favorite haunts, and she did not leave that evening until half past six. But she did not see how the president's wife often simply annoyed him with her relentless personality and analyzed the problem not as the annoyance, together with wifely inattention before and after an affair of twenty-five years earlier, but concluded that "Mrs. R." lacked only one thing: the ability to relax and play with her husband. The more she thought about that explanation, she wrote in her diary, the more it seemed right.[11]

It is a pity that at this crucial time in her husband's life Eleanor Roosevelt could not have done more for him—but it was an impossibly complicated situation. Years later Dr. Bruenn made it seem too simple. He said, quite correctly, that the president's wife gave her husband no attention. He believed that in the worsening of her husband's illness she had much to answer for. He told former secretary of the interior Ickes, who inquired, that Mrs. Roosevelt had no concern or even interest in seeing to it that the president had the care a man in his situation required. Ickes, the self-styled "curmudgeon" (he titled his 1943 memoirs *The Autobiography of a Curmudgeon*), was equally unsympathetic toward Mrs. Roosevelt; after an unsatisfactory marriage he had married a pretty young woman who brought him much happiness. But the physician and former secretary were a little hard on the president's wife. The Roosevelts' marriage was not made in heaven, and by the time of World War II its problems could not be remedied. The problems could be traced back to the childhoods of both partners. Husband and wife had grown up pampered and spoiled by money and too much breeding as it then was known. They married too soon to sense the meaning of love, beyond having six children in rapid succession (one died in infancy). The husband was uncaring and busy; the wife felt sorry for herself, although she passed off most of the child rearing to servants. Then came the real trouble. When Lucy Mercer, socially well bred but poor, pert and pretty as a picture, barely out of her teens, settled into the household she was both a temptation and an impossibility. The marriage could not be broken because of the size of the family, the religious issue (Lucy was a devout Catholic and could not marry a divorced man), Roosevelt's political ambitions, and the objections of his mother, the former Sara Delano, who controlled the family purse strings. The mother was against a divorce for good Episcopalian and other reasons, but did not scruple to poison what was left of the marriage. Anna remembered how "Granny" pampered the grandchildren to get them on her side and many times at the Hyde Park dinner table related how "Franklin" could have married "so many pretty girls." On each such pronouncement her daughter-in-law would leave the table in tears. Her husband said nothing. The children took the side of the grandmother. Only later did they come to see that Granny was just an "old bitch."[12]

As February 1944 passed into March, hope arose that the president would recover quickly from his illness; people around the ailing chief executive began to feel that his illness was receding. The Hyde Park trips allowed for less rigmarole than remaining in the White House, and visitors diminished markedly. Everything was fairly simple. The president could send his secretary, Grace G. Tully, and her assistant, Dorothy Brady, to the Nelson House in Poughkeepsie where they could keep company with Press Secretary Early and the reporters. The trio—Tully, Brady, and Early—were familiar figures to the president; Tully was the efficient successor to Marguerite, or Missy, LeHand who had suffered a stroke, Brady her typist, and Early an able former reporter. Secret Service men also were around but tried to be less conspicuous, and soldiers guarding Hyde Park were lost in the shrubbery and the expanse of road leading to the mansion. In such surroundings the president seemed better, and Hassett, who was as worshipful as Daisy, wrote on February 20, a Tuesday, that "The President much benefited, as usual, from his stay in the old home, where he had been sleeping ten hours a night while his enemies have supposed he was lying awake nights worrying about their machinations." On March 2, Daisy wrote that the president was feverish and generally miserable and looked bad as he lay on a sofa. She and Anna, who had accompanied him from Washington, put pillows behind him and a light cover on top. They took his temperature, which was 100½, and called the doctor, who said to give him two aspirins and soda. Daisy told her diary it was "just a reaction from the tooth pulling"—the president had lost a tooth that was so loose it almost fell out.[13]

But then Daisy was invited down to Washington and on Sunday, March 19, found him in bed again with a temperature a little more than 100. It could have been the weather, which was dreary, rain on top of snow. Perhaps it was return of the flu. "I'm inclined to think these headaches of his are from indigestion," she wrote. She thought he needed cleaning out, his whole system, for he ate too much and too rich food. On March 20 she had a quiet supper with him, on a tray, and for once it was sensible: raw oysters, tomato soup, and Sanka. This abstention may have been why she could write on March 23 that "The P. is gradually getting over his illness; he has had no fever for two days, has been eating rightly & got up for tea yesterday."[14] She hoped to solve everything by some mineral salts she had received and about which the president had promised to talk to McIntire. She had gotten in touch with a French healer, Grace Gassette, whose stock-in-trade was boxes of salts of a homeopathic sort. Mlle Gassette had allegedly cured many cases of paralysis in France of twenty years' standing; in France she consulted and worked with physicians, and Daisy believed she could work wonders with the ill president. Unfortunately the admiral sent the salts out to Bethesda for analysis, and they turned out to be worthless, although they might have caused what Daisy described as a cleaning out.

By this time, despite the appearance of nothing being done or about to be done, something at long last was about to be done. The president's condition appeared to be more than postflu. Hassett began to sense it, and on March 24 saw the president in his bedroom, where he often did business with his principal secretaries in mornings. FDR was not looking well. Later at a press and radio conference his voice was husky and off pitch. Every morning, in response to Hassett's polite inquiries as to how he felt, the president was answering "rotten" or "like hell."[15] Anna Roosevelt, who possessed a considerable decisiveness, therefore spoke to Dr. McIntire about her father's illness and insisted that he bring in consultants. What she said to him has never become clear. McIntire seems to have taken her suggestion with ill humor, yet the request was reasonable enough and he had little choice except to go along, if only because if she went to her father she could have caused trouble. Her father adored her, with good reason, for of the five surviving Roosevelt children (Anna was the oldest, followed by four sons) she was the only one who gave him real attention. Some years later Steve Early told Ickes that the other family members were all "out for themselves," and only Anna had shown both affection and good judgment.[16]

In advance of the physical examination ordered by McIntire at the request of Anna the president made another trip to Hyde Park, with no better result than the recent trips. Sunday, March 26, with little mail in the pouch from the White House, he said he had a good night's rest and his appetite was only fair. There was a little fever in the morning—it usually came on at night. But in the evening Grace Tully telephoned from Hyde Park where she was staying that the president was feeling worse, with a temperature of 104, and was ordering the train in readiness to go back the next morning, March 27, at eleven o'clock in the morning, rather than leave on the evening of that day. Anna had lined up the physical examination at Bethesda for the following morning, March 28, and it was better to leave earlier. Hassett noticed that when the president arrived at Highland to board the train on Monday, he looked worn and ill. He said he felt all right then, but guessed the temperature would come back in the evening. He mentioned the checkup the next day. The train arrived at the bureau terminal at half past six, and the president at once went to the White House and had supper in bed.

The next morning came the so-called head-to-toe examination, and it is interesting that despite the claim in McIntire's book that the president frequently had such examinations one might wonder— there is now no way to be sure—how many of these he really had during the eleven years of his presidency as of March 28, 1944. It is entirely possible that the examination of that fateful morning constituted the first serious consultation Admiral McIntire ever had ordered. An indication that this might have been the case is that when Dr. Bruenn learned that he was to see professionally the president of the United States he received no records of previous examinations— he did not obtain the pertinent part or any parts at all of his new patient's chart. He insisted to McIntire that he must know his patient's history, and with reluctance the admiral had the chart sent for, and it arrived in the middle of Bruenn's examination of the president.

Most fortunately the cardiac examination on Tuesday, March 28, 1944, was in the hands of a specialist of thorough competence. Had a less competent physician been assigned to the case, or if Anna Roosevelt had not been willing to force Admiral McIntire to a consultation and the admiral remained in charge, it is entirely possible that the president might have died in 1944. The then vice president, Henry A. Wallace, would have become president, instead of the man who took Wallace's place in the short-lived Roosevelt fourth term, that is, Harry S. Truman. With Wallace as president, a man who had never run for public office save for the vice presidency in 1940, and who later was seen to have had very limited understanding of American politics, and who in foreign policy flirted with a reconciliation with the Soviet Union of Joseph Stalin during the early years of the Cold War, 1945–1948, when he was for some months secretary of commerce and then formed his own political party and campaigned for the presidency in 1948: with Wallace as president in 1944 the Cold War might have gone much differently than it did, might not have happened, with the world a strikingly different place.

Fortunately for the future the president received the best medical science of that time. Bruenn was thirty-nine years of age, and had graduated in 1929 from Johns Hopkins Medical School where he studied with men who were leading specialists during the first generation of American medical science, who themselves had been young men in the 1880s and 1890s. The present writer met Bruenn when the doctor was in his eighties. Of medium height, powerfully built, face marked by sympathetic, friendly eyes and an almost boyish grin, he reminisced fondly about the first-class people at Hopkins when he was in training, such men as the urologist Hugh H. Young who attended President Wilson (and who in February 1920 revealed the truth about Wilson's stroke to a reporter). Before the war Bruenn had been a resident and member of the faculty at perhaps the best hospital in New York City, Columbia Presbyterian. At the time of Pearl Harbor he went to a recruiting station and sought to enlist in the navy, to be told that if he waited until his thirty-eighth birthday, the next year, he would be brought in as a lieutenant commander instead of a lieutenant junior grade. He waited, and upon commissioning with the higher rank on October 29, 1942, was sent to an upstate New York hospital where he began seeing all sorts of cases. Then for reasons he never understood—for assignments for specialist physicians in the navy were well known to be peculiar, with neurosurgeons becoming obstetricians and vice versa, the old-line medical corps officers assigning personnel as if any training was the same as any other—expecting the worst Bruenn received the best, for he was transferred to the navy's premier hospital near the capital, Bethesda, as head of the Electrocardiograph Department and consultant to the Third Naval District. Any officer up for promotion who might have cardiac problems was sent to Bruenn.

On the morning of March 28 at Bethesda the Electrocardiograph Department was understandably on edge when down the corridor to its examining rooms came the wheelchair of the president, who was smiling and as jocular as ever, and to whom Bruenn introduced himself and the members of his staff. Retiring to a dressing room the president was readied and brought out to the examining table, and Bruenn and staff members helped lift him up on the table for the examination. At that very moment Bruenn was shocked, for he saw that the president was short of breath.

As the examination proceeded, everything went downhill, from bad to worse. Part of the way through the examination the chart arrived, and the cardiologist excused himself for a hasty reading, which showed a steady rise in systolic and diastolic blood pressures. The pressures Bruenn took that day were clearly dangerous, 186/108.[17] Fluoroscopy and X rays of the chest showed a large increase in the heart shadow in the anterior-posterior position. Enlargement of the heart was mainly of the left ventricle, the pumping chamber. There were no palpable thrills, the heart rhythm was regular, but percussion showed the heart's apex in the sixth interspace, two centimeters to the left of the midclavicular line. At the end of the examination Bruenn diagnosed hypertension, hypertensive heart disease, cardiac failure (left ventricular), and—the sole instance in which Admiral McIntire had been correct—acute bronchitis.

Many years later Jan Kenneth Herman, editor of the navy's general journal for the Bureau of Medicine and Surgery, *Navy Medicine,* asked Bruenn if the president's problem had been lack of exercise because of the polio, twelve years of unremitting stress, or diet. "It was the high blood pressure," was the response. Herman asked Bruenn about the condition in which he found the president on March 28, 1944. "He was in heart failure," was the answer. The danger was that a sudden high of pressure might reach out for the well-known target areas, which were the heart, kidneys, and brain. Bruenn told his interviewer, and later said the same thing to the present writer, that the president's condition was "God-awful."[18]

2

When it came to analyzing what was wrong with President Roosevelt, what ailed him, the president himself was not of much assistance. On March 28, the same day he had his physical examination and Dr. Bruenn discovered him in heart failure, he returned to the White House and held a press conference, during which a reporter asked how he felt and reminded him of the rumors that his health had not been very good. FDR responded that he had bronchitis but otherwise was fine. He said the bronchitis was not very serious, that he had been told that 1 out of 48,500 cases of bronchitis developed into pneumonia, and so he thought he had rather a slim chance. At the conference he made a point about his wife. "I can't think of anything else that has happened the last few days," he related, "except that about half an hour ago Mrs. Roosevelt got back from South America."[19]

The same day he telephoned Daisy Suckley to report on the doctors' exams of the morning, and went into more detail. He said they took X rays and all sorts of tests, found nothing drastically wrong, and one sinus was clogged up. The physicians, he told Daisy, were going to put him on a strict diet, which Daisy described to her diary as a good beginning. She asked him ("begged him," she said) to get back on what she seemingly had prescribed weeks or even months before, lemon juice in hot water before breakfast. He said he might, which—although Daisy did not remark it—meant he would not. He reported to her that a doctor, perhaps it was McIntire, told him the previous week that he had elevated levels of uric acid.[20]

Nor was Admiral McIntire more helpful in giving out the truth about the president's condition—although McIntire soon knew a good deal more than did his distinguished patient. On March 30, reporters asked Press Secretary Early if it would be possible to make public the results of the president's physical examination. Early incautiously replied that it might be, as soon as the report was received from the hospital. On April 4, Admiral McIntire came into Early's press conference to report that Roosevelt's health was "satisfactory." The *New York Times* announced that what the admiral subsequently said amounted to an unprecedented report on the presidential visit to Bethesda. McIntire said that the president had been suffering for a month from a head cold and bronchitis, and also had influenza or "respiratory infection" together with a sinus disturbance. At one point he referred to "this acute flare-up of his sinuses and chest." "When we got through," he said of the Bethesda checkup, "we decided that for a man of 62-plus we had very little to argue about, with the exception that we have had to combat the influenza plus the respiratory complications that came along after." He said the president had been put on a vitamin-rich diet and left the impression Roosevelt needed sunshine and more exercise. With that, "then I wouldn't complain." "The bronchitis had made him a little hoarse, and I felt if we could hold him in his study for his work, and not run him from room to room where temperature changes occur, we would clean this thing up." The physical checkup, he said, was a yearly event and was "very complete." "I can say to you," he declared,

> that the checkup is satisfactory. The only thing that we need to finish up on is just the residuals of this bronchitis and one of his sinuses, and they are clearing very rapidly. He is feeling quite well this morning. In fact, I think, he will be getting out today. The greatest criticism we can have is the fact that we haven't been able to provide him with enough exercise and sunshine. Now that is something we have lacked right along, in this press of things. So that would be my criticism of myself and all the rest of us who have to run this establishment around here, that we haven't been able to provide him with the right kind of routine.[21]

All the while, in those last days of March, early days of April, Bruenn's findings were creating an uproar—albeit within the precincts of Bethesda. The first set-to came when the cardiologist, who could hardly get over his shock at what he had discovered, reported to Admiral McIntire that the president's condition required digitalis immediately, together with bed rest and a careful diet. McIntire turned wrathful ("S.G. somewhat unprintable when notified").[22] "You can't do that," he said, and perhaps even shouted. "This is the President of the United States!"[23] Bruenn, normally a calm man, and assuredly a man with considerable backbone, based on his training and position at Columbia Presbyterian, seems to have looked the red-faced admiral in the eye, perhaps not even seeing McIntire's broad admiral's stripe, and insisted on his diagnosis.

There was nothing for McIntire to do, having gotten himself into this situation because the president's daughter asked for a consultation, but to convene a board, composed of himself and the staff heads at Bethesda. The board assembled two days after Bruenn had seen the president, on March 30, and Bruenn acquainted its members with his findings. Present were McIntire, Bruenn, Capts. John Harper, Robert Duncan, and Charles Behrens, respectively commandant, executive officer, and head of radiology at Bethesda, and a local consultant,

Paul Dickens, clinical professor of medicine at George Washington University.

Next day, March 31, the same group met, together with two more consultants mentioned earlier, Drs. Lahey and Paullin. Bruenn found himself virtually fighting it out against the assembled officers and consultants, all of whom sought to pooh-pooh (his word) his diagnosis.[24] The consensus was that he was overwrought, that he was desiring to prescribe too much. The diet was the least of the problem. The proposed digitalization of the president was excessive. As for bed rest, treating the president as if he were an ill man confined like a hospital patient or someone in a convalescent home—that was impossible.

Bruenn faced up to the board at this second meeting, with the serene confidence that his navy service was a temporary and not altogether crucial portion of his medical career. He insisted on his own judgment. As he looked around the table he could see a good deal less than met the eye. He had encountered plenty of expertise when at Hopkins and at his teaching hospital, but who were these people? McIntire he already had calculated, for the admiral had made a gross misdiagnosis, one that might have brought serious action at Columbia Presbyterian. Harper and Duncan were administrative people. Behrens was head of radiology. Lahey was "a very able surgeon and by reputation a prominent one." Paullin was an internist, a "good doctor, definitely, but very politically inclined. Anybody that becomes president of the AMA has spent a long time in the hierarchy of committees and so forth. You don't get picked out of the group to become president. You have to work for it."[25]

Secure in his diagnosis Bruenn argued his position. He stressed that because of the physical limits of the patient, Roosevelt's inability to walk and therefore exercise in any strenuous way that might reveal his cardiovascular condition, the "usual history of a diminished myocardial reserve" was not possible to obtain. The patient himself, when Bruenn asked him about his illnesses, had spoken vaguely, but said enough to make the cardiologist sense a history of orthopnea, namely, that breathing was better when the president sat in an erect position rather than lay on a sofa or bed. Bruenn, too, when he helped lift Roosevelt onto the examining table had noticed the dyspnea, or labored breathing. Then there was the size of the heart, sensed by percussing the chest. The X ray showed hilar congestion, that is, at the part of the heart where blood vessels and nerves entered. The few functional tests performed all indicated "the presence of definite congestive heart failure."[26]

On the afternoon of March 31, after the second meeting of the board, Drs. Lahey and Paullin went over to the White House and examined the president. Lahey, Bruenn reported years later, was particularly interested in the gastrointestinal tract but believed (contrary to the missing Lahey memorandum) there was no need for surgical procedure. Lahey did say that he thought the situation was serious enough to warrant acquainting the president with the full facts of the case, so as to secure his full cooperation.

At a third board meeting on the morning of April 1 the consensus was that Bruenn could go ahead and digitalize the president. It was agreed upon only after the cardiologist said during the discussions that if the board would not assent to his interpretation of the president's illness and follow his proposals, he wished to have nothing more to do with the case. Lahey said at this point that "this is out of my field," a remark Bruenn appreciated.[27] Paullin in a sort of political manner remarked being fully in accord with the diagnosis but he did not believe congestive heart failure was present in sufficient degree to require digitalization; he suggested doing nothing, use of no therapy.

Taking over, after what to another individual might have been a harrowing experience with the board, Bruenn digitalized the president and in a week or ten days, as he told Jan Herman, "the results were spectacular."[28] Roosevelt's lungs, which had been congested and contained a small amount of fluid, were now clear. His heart had diminished in size. The coughing stopped, and he slept soundly at night. The consultants came back a few days later, and the changes in the patient were so dramatic that the members of the board could hardly deny Bruenn's professional competence. Even the admiral was convinced. During the board sessions he had said, in admiral fashion, "No problem, things are not that bad."[29] Now they were undeniably improved. Bruenn wrote on April 3:

> Pt. had a very refreshing night's sleep (10 hours and had to be awakened in a.m.). P.E. [physical examination]—Color good. Not dyspneic lying flat. Did not cough during entire examination. Lungs—Entirely clear. Heart—For the first time a distinct

impulse can be observed in the 6th i.s. [interspace] in the left anterior axillary line. Palpation over this area reveals a strong forceful impact. The first sound at the apex has a much better tone than formerly but is still followed by a systolic blow. The systolic murmur at the base persists. B.P. 208/108.

On April 4, "Another excellent night. No complaints except that he feels that he has been eating too much—'getting fat' (diet is only 1,800 calories). No gastric discomfort. P.E.—Looks much better. Color good. Lies flat with dyspnea. Lungs—Clear thruout. Heart—Unchanged. Sounds are clear and strong. B.P.—222-226/118. Has cut down appreciably on his tobacco (6 cigarettes a day)." On April 5 things were still going much better. "In excellent spirits. Slept well. Still thinks that he has too much to eat. No G.I. complaints but is afraid of getting 'fat.' Feels fine. Coughs very little. P.E.—Looks well. Lungs—Clear. Heart—First sound at the apex is now of normal tone and louder than the second in this area. Apical impulse vigorous. Apical & basal systolic murmurs as before. No diastolic murmurs heard. B.P. 218/120." On April 6 the signs were good. "A very good night. Complained of a little 'nausea' yesterday in the late afternoon. When questioned, however, dismissed it as of no account. Ate his dinner last night and his breakfast this morning with relish. No other complaints. Cough has practically disappeared. P.E.—Looks very well. Lungs—Clear. H[ear]t.—Unchanged. Good heart sounds and vigorous pulsations persist. B.P. 210/120."

The above diary comments by the president's cardiologist deserve some explanation. At the outset of taking over with the president Bruenn began a diary of his experiences, and continued it for a short while on a daily basis, then intermittently, until his distinguished patient's death the next year. The beginning of the diary is in the form of a hospital chart, but as the diary progresses it becomes more personal. The opening comments for March 28 (misdated in their handwritten form as March 27) and until the end of the month and a bit more, when he began digitalization, give the appearance of having been written a few days after the events they describe, but the diary settles into entries written the same day. Altogether there are sixty-three. From the outset, from a sense of history in the making, also a feeling that he had better keep his own record, the cardiologist made these entries. Each day after taking over care of the president he wrote in Roosevelt's chart, a separate record, kept in the safe at Bethesda. When the chart disappeared Bruenn thus had his own record and was able eventually, in 1970, to publish his definitive account of Roosevelt's illness in the *Annals of Internal Medicine*.[30] The diary became available to historical researchers after Bruenn's death in 1995, when his widow deposited a small box of his papers in the Roosevelt Library at Hyde Park.

In the above-quoted diary entries the reader will notice the president's concern about getting fat. One of the principal problems Bruenn faced in treating his distinguished patient was Roosevelt's worry about overeating. In the past he had enjoyed food, and ate everything in sight. He liked rich food and was overweight, considering that although he was tall, six feet two, all his weight was in his stomach and shoulders, his hips and legs having atrophied. Like most people who are overweight he worried about the weight but did little about it. The weight was none too good for his cardiovascular system, and Bruenn put him on a diet. At first he hated the diet. As months passed he began to like the loss of weight, and cooperated too much with it. He became almost anorexic. In addition, his increasing illness subtracted from his former substantial appetite. Bruenn had to take him off the diet and try to find no-fat substitutes. All the while the president bragged to anyone who would listen about his "flat tummy" and took pride in his more youthful figure that looked back to the years before the attack of poliomyelitis forced him to forego the exercise that had kept him thin.

In one entry for April 6, Bruenn wrote that the president went for an automobile drive that afternoon and keenly enjoyed it, and added an explanation about the digitalis, "omitted today." Roosevelt had shown gastric discomfort. The difficulty with digitalis was its toxicity. The therapeutic range was narrow. A sign of overdigitalization was loss of appetite; when a patient complained, the physician had to pull back.

On April 7 everything again was all right: "No complaints. Looks and feels very well. P.E.—Essentially unchanged. B.P. 208/ 114. . . . Pt. was seen by Drs. Lahey and Paullin with Admiral McIntire."

During the examination of March 28 at Bethesda, Bruenn had received Roosevelt's chart and looked it over hurriedly, and after he became virtually the president's physician he had more time to examine it, and found it not very informative. McIntire in the book of 1946 was explicit about head-to-toe physical examinations, but the chart did not reveal them; it did not offer the detail such exams would have required. Nor were there many blood pressure readings. Bruenn said to some of the historians who came to see him that it was not customary in the 1930s to take blood pressure readings. These standard items in examinations today, even the most cursory, were not staples of the medical profession at that time.

The lack of blood pressure readings in Roosevelt's chart raises a very interesting point in the history of medicine in this century. It showed how general medical practice was at that time, how only in large and up-to-date hospitals, such as Bruenn's in New York, had physicians turned to specialties beyond the time-honored ones—general surgery, neurology, and obstetrics. Cardiology had become a specialty only in the early 1920s, about the time when Paul Dudley White began his Boston practice. The first diagnosis of a heart attack had occurred in 1910 when a Chicago physician, James B. Herrick, diagnosed a cardiac infarction in a fifty-five-year-old banker who after a moderate meal suffered chest pain and acute indigestion and died fifty-two hours later. When the pathologist asked where to look for the trouble, Herrick said he would find a clot in one of the coronary arteries, which turned out exactly to be the problem. In the early 1920s, Dr. Samuel A. Levine of Boston's Peter Bent Brigham Hospital diagnosed the first heart attack in a patient who survived. Of the five physicians who attended President Warren G. Harding at San Francisco in 1923, including a former president and the current president of the AMA, none suspected the heart attack that killed him instantly, in seconds, all misdiagnosing the patient as dying of apoplexy, a stroke, which would have required at least ten minutes. And so during the 1930s another president of the United States was attended by a physician and by "our Navy specialists," perhaps once in a while "famous consultants," who were no more skilled in cardiology than Harding's physicians. Bruenn realized full well that cardiology was not represented in the hospital chart of the president.

The few blood pressure readings that Bruenn saw or learned about, prior to his examination, were nonetheless unsettling. The physical examination made available to reporters in 1931 showed pressure of 140/100, a mild but important elevation above the norm, 120/80. There was an abnormal electrocardiograph indicating enlargement of the left side of the heart and displaying an inversion of the T waves in Lead 3, usually meaning a decrease in blood flow to the heart. The chart contained only a few blood pressure readings, and they were no more encouraging. A reading of July 30, 1935, was all right, 136/78. Another of April 22, 1937, was not, 162/98. Thereafter the numbers rose, one or the other or both. On November 13, 1940, it was 178/88. On February 27, 1941, it was 188/105. The present writer remarked upon the systolic of that last reading to Dr. Bruenn, who responded, "And the diastolic was going up too." The diastolic rise meant more than the already hypertensive systolic. The so-called diastole is the rhythmical expansion of cavities of the heart as they fill with blood, and hence marks the force being exerted upon the arteries.

And what to say about the 186/108 that Bruenn found on March 28, 1944? The medical historian Dr. Park went to *Cecil's Textbook of Medicine*, 1944 edition, and read what Admiral McIntire could have read, had the navy's surgeon general not been so occupied with administrative duties: "In malignant hypertension, the systolic blood pressure is excessively high, 200 to 250 mm, and the diastolic pressure is correspondingly elevated. Retinal hemorrhage . . . and congestive heart failure commonly complicate the clinical picture and cerebral vascular accidents are not infrequent. The condition is invariably fatal." In a 1980s edition of *Cecil's Textbook*, Dr. Park quoted an equally graphic account, this of statistics relating to high blood pressure: "Comparing normotensive individuals with those having a pressure exceeding 160 systolic and 95 diastolic mm Hg [Park interpolated, "values with which McIntire was apparently comfortable"] the [increased risk] is three-fold for coronary disease, four-fold for congestive heart failure, and seven-fold for stroke."[31]

In later years when he thought back over the president's condition as he discovered it, Dr. Bruenn wondered when things had begun to fall apart. It was so difficult to know. Perhaps it was only a few years earlier. The president himself, because of his immobility, his being either in the wheelchair or lifted, was of little help. Here he was, not in desperate but surely in critical condition, and he had not realized it. McIntire's concerns—sinus problems, influenza, and bronchitis—had been far off the mark; there had been no help from that side. In an interview with the historian Brenda L. Heaster,

Dorothy Bruenn, a nurse, intervened: "But he was really out of his depth anyway." "All the time," responded her husband.[32]

The great danger, as Bruenn and *Cecil's Textbook* in 1944 testified to and forty years later the textbook gave statistics about, was that the high blood pressure would affect the target areas. The involvement of the heart and kidneys was "greatly advanced, you see. It was time to do something about it." The pressure involved "the brain, you see." Like Presidents Wilson and Harding, the first suffering a major stroke, the second a fatal heart attack, Roosevelt could look forward to something that Bruenn after the event described as a "pop."[33]

Like Roosevelt's predecessor presidents, there was little that medical science, short of immediate retirement from the presidency, could have done to assist him. Asked if there was any medication for hypertension in 1944, Bruenn responded with an immediate "No." He told Herman, "We tried to cut down on his weight, and to reduce stress, be sure he got a good night's sleep, cut down on salt—the usual things. But there was nothing directly to control it." In 1969 the president's daughter wrote to Bruenn, who was about to publish his article, to say that her then husband, Dr. James A. Halsted, had mentioned the difference that might have occurred "in Father's case" if antihypertensive drugs had been available in those days as they were for President Dwight D. Eisenhower who suffered a major heart attack in 1955 and for Lyndon B. Johnson who suffered a similar attack the same year, being then a senator. Unfortunately for Roosevelt the drugs were not yet developed. Looking back, in 1989, Bruenn remarked that the change in treatment of high blood pressure had been extraordinary. "We had nothing like that in those days—nothing." If it only had been possible to get the blood pressure down,

> if we could have done it, we would have taken all the stress off all his arteries, including his primary arteries as well as the cerebral when he finally died. So, it was a tragedy that we couldn't do anything about blood pressure particularly. Except the things which were usually good for those things—protect him from stress, keep down his excitement, insist on him having rest after lunch and that sort of business, cutting his weight down. Those were the only methods available. Now, good Lord, there are dozens of medications which are so effective.[34]

That, then, was the meaning of the horrifying discovery of March 28, 1944.

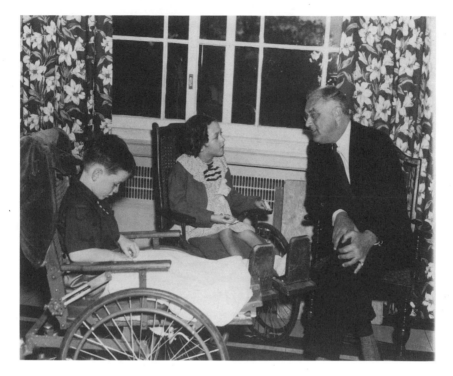

Undated. Young patients at Warm Springs chat with the president.
National Archives.

Undated, 1944. With Fala at Hill-Top Cottage, a part of the estate at Hyde Park. Photographed by Margaret Suckley. *Franklin D. Roosevelt Library.*

February 26, 1944. Driving the Ford Phaeton, in the woods at Hyde Park. *Franklin D. Roosevelt Library.*

July 19, 1944. Inspecting amphibious training, Oceanside, California.
National Archives.

July 20, 1944. San Diego. Broadcasting acceptance of nomination by the Democratic convention in Chicago. Right: Colonel James Roosevelt and wife. *Franklin D. Roosevelt Library.*

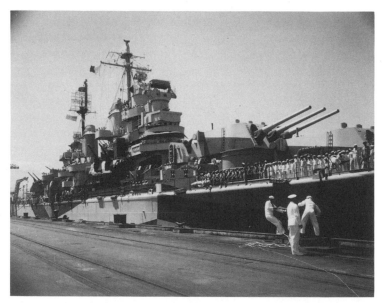

July 26, 1944. The heavy cruiser USS *Baltimore* arrives at Pearl Harbor, flying the presidential flag. *National Archives.*

July 26, 1944. General MacArthur, the president, Admiral Nimitz. Standing at rear left is Admiral Ross T. McIntire, between the president and Nimitz is Samuel I. Rosenman. *Franklin D. Roosevelt Library.*

July 28, 1944. Honolulu. Conference on Pacific strategy. General MacArthur, the president, Admirals Nimitz and Leahy. *National Archives.*

July 28, 1944. Conference on Pacific strategy. *National Archives.*

Inspecting troops, with Lieutenant General Robert C. Richardson and Admiral Leahy. *National Archives.*

August 7, 1944. The president fishes at a small lake on Kodiak Island.
Franklin D. Roosevelt Library.

August 18, 1944. Luncheon outside the White House with his vice-presidential running mate. *Harry S. Truman Library.*

September 11, 1944. Wolfe's Cove Railroad Station, Quebec. With Prime Minister Churchill. *Franklin D. Roosevelt Library.*

September 12, 1944. On the terrace of the Citadel, Quebec. Left to right: the Earl of Athlone, governor general of Canada; the president; Prime Minister Churchill; W. L. Mackenzie King, prime minister of Canada.
Franklin D. Roosevelt Library.

September 16, 1944. Meeting the press at Quebec.
Franklin D. Roosevelt Library.

October 5, 1944. In a campaign speech the president assails the "reckless words" of his enemies. *Franklin D. Roosevelt Library.*

October 27, 1944. The president visits the Philadelphia Navy
Yard. *Franklin D. Roosevelt Library.*

October 27, 1944. Addressing crowd at City Hall Plaza, Camden, New Jersey.
Franklin D. Roosevelt Library.

October 28, 1944. Soldiers' Field, Chicago. "Those same quarrelsome, tired old men—they have built the greatest military machine the world has ever known . . ." *Franklin D. Roosevelt Library.*

November 10, 1944. Union Station, Washington. With Vice President–Elect Harry S. Truman and Vice President Henry A. Wallace.
Franklin D. Roosevelt Library.

December 18, 1944. Returning from his second-to-last visit to Warm Springs, the president inspects marines at Camp Lejeune, North Carolina. He is talking with Captain Herbert S. Gibson. *National Archives.*

Reviewing marines at Lejeune, December 18, 1944. *National Archives.*

*T*he months from April through December 1944 might be described as a time of adjustment, when whatever news the president discovered about his incapacity he learned to live with. After he chose a vice presidential running mate for his fourth campaign for the presidency, he went to Hawaii to get away from things. He came back to several months of relative routine.

But increasingly the work of keeping going was awkward; it was tempting to let details go so long as appearances were all right. One can sense no Rooseveltian exuberance, none of the joy that marked earlier years in the White House. The impression one obtains is that during this time everything was dull and uninspiring; the present held few novelties and no challenges; he had seen it all before.

In this atmosphere of everything becoming smaller the election of November 1944 seems to have been little more than a ripple, an event ordained by the Constitution and therefore necessary, but nothing that took much of the presidential energy. At the Quebec Conference in September with Prime Minister Churchill and with the Canadian prime minister, W. L. Mackenzie King, the president was concerned that he might not be reelected. He said that voting of servicemen depended on individual states and that several states would not allow servicemen to vote. He was bothered by the talk of his Republican opponent that year, Gov. Thomas E. Dewey of New York, that he was too old, incapable of handling the tasks of the war, not to mention those of the approaching peace. The Republicans said the president was "a senile old man."[1] On October 30, 1944, the president's appointments secretary, Maj. Gen. Edwin M., or Pa, Watson, advised Budget Director Smith, who was coming in for an appointment, to talk politics with FDR. Watson was close to Roosevelt. He gave the impression of a bumbling, overpromoted military man decorating the presidential outer office, overweight and unobservant, but was nothing of the sort. He knew FDR's worries and especially the worry about Dewey, who was a real challenger. He told Smith, concerning Dewey, that "we are going to lick that little lying bastard."[2] But then, after all the discussion, the president did the usual thing: showed his invincible ability as a campaigner. He made the "Fala" speech, poking fun at the Republican claim that he had sent a destroyer one thousand miles to Alaska to bring back the president's Scottie, which had been left behind. With that single speech, in which he said that he did not mind the Republican canard but Fala did (Fala was Scotch, his Scotch soul was furious, he "has not been the same dog since"), he set the tone of the campaign, and thereafter had only to show himself in the rain throughout the boroughs of New York and make excursions to Philadelphia, Chicago, and Boston, and victory was ensured.

1

The new regime insisted upon by Dr. Bruenn, insofar as he could insist, was marked not merely by the life-giving digitalis but by an attempt to put the president on a diet, with which the nation's chief executive at first was not very happy. On April 2, 1944, he called up Daisy Suckley at Rhinebeck (he was at Hyde Park) to let her know what he just had eaten, scrambled eggs and rice and milk, this for supper. He said that generally speaking, although the time was too short to register any result from the diet and whatever else the doctors were doing, he felt about the same as before.

The conversation was interesting in what it said between the lines, which was that he still did not much understand his condition. He told Daisy he really had pneumonia. Daisy felt immediately that the doctors were not doing their best for the pneumonia, since they had let him, or he had let himself, go around Hyde Park in his open car the preceding Sunday and sit in one of the estate's cottages when the inside was chilly. She wrote sternly in her diary that a member of the family, presumably herself, *should be with him* (italics hers) all the time. During the conversation the president told Daisy he expected to get off on Tuesday. Daisy suspected, and Roosevelt may have said as much, the reason was to wait another twenty-four hours for the bronchial tubes to clear up. She observed that while in Hyde Park he was getting up at about noon, went to his desk in the study to eat his lunch, worked with Grace Tully, and went back to bed at six. This meant a four-hour workday, not too large for a president of the United States in wartime, with D-Day in Europe two months away and the Pacific campaigns coming that summer, the occupation of Saipan allowing the new heavy bombers, the B-29s, close access to the home islands. Gen. Douglas MacArthur would follow with invasion of the Philippines ("I shall return") in the autumn. Relating the president's work hours the diarist concluded that her cousin felt so tired, all the time, but then, "That is not strange, considering that he has walking pneumonia."[3]

The return to Washington took place, and Saturday, April 8, the president again left the capital for what would prove a month of rest, in accord with his doctors' prescription, at the South Carolina estate of Baruch. Roosevelt spent twenty-eight days at Hobcaw, arriving April 9 and departing May 6. He intended to stay two weeks, the reporters were told, but liked the place so much he stayed four.

If any locale could have lent itself to helping the president's condition, Hobcaw was the place. Distant from the local railroad station, twenty-three thousand acres, with a large fireproof brick house sprawling in front of Winyah Bay, it was as restful a place as anyone might have hoped to find. The president fished from a pier jutting out toward Hare and Rabbit Islands. Everywhere were pines, cypresses, and live oaks festooned with Spanish moss. The "barony," as it was known, had been granted to Lord Carteret, one of the lord proprietors of Carolina, in 1718. Baruch bought it in 1905. He had only a few acres in cultivation, but employed forty people, maintaining for them a small village, complete with school, church, and cemetery. Adjoining the plantation was Bellefield, owned by his daughter, Belle. To the north was the acreage of George Vanderbilt, who was on active service in the army. To the south was the land of Thomas Yawkey, proprietor of the Boston Red Sox.

There was little to distract the president. The pool reporters, only three newspapermen, were eight miles away, in the Prince George Hotel at Georgetown. Marines stood guard at all entrances or exits to the plantation and surrounded the house. During the president's stay Baruch was present; he was not about to miss the company his hospitality made possible. Baruch's daughter appeared from time to time. The president had in a few friends or administration officials. Otherwise it was staff members and not many of them. At Hobcaw the president's daily schedule was as follows: arise, 11:30 a.m.; lunch, 1:00 p.m.; nap, 2:00 to 4:00; outing, 4:00 to 6:30; dinner, 8:00; to bed, 9.00.[4]

Bruenn's diary recorded the Hobcaw weeks.

4-17-44 Patient appears to be very well and in good spirits. He has been sleeping soundly—"I sleep too much"—and has eaten well. He disclaims any great appetite but it has been noted that he eats all of his portions of food. Has complained intermittently of abdominal gas—but no nausea. No cardiac symptoms. P.E.—Essentially unchanged. Lungs are clear. B.P. 206/116.

4-18-44 Cough has practically disappeared. He does complain of thick mucous in the back of his throat and not infrequently has to clear it. P.E. As before. B.P. 220/120. Vitamins (Unicaps) t.i.d. [*ter in die*, thrice a day] started. A review of the B.P. readings obtained during the past few days reveals no significant change in the levels. Accordingly, it has been suggested that the Thesodate which has been given is not effective. It was stopped. KI—drips. B.i.d. begun. [Thesodate is a caffeinelike compound of theobromine sodium acetate that increases the heart rate, but may raise blood pressure; KI is potassium iodide, used as an expectorant, often found in cough mixtures; b.i.d. is *bis in die*, twice a day.]

4-19 and 4-20-44 Observations over this period of time reveal the very interesting fact that there is a marked diurnal change in the B.P. Unlike the usual variation, the highest B.P. readings have invariably been recorded in the morning, the lowest in the evening. When the blood pressure was taken before breakfast and with the patient still in a prone position, B.P. was found to be 230/126–128. One hour later, the B.P. was 210/106. The only activity during this interval was for the patient to sit up and eat his breakfast. After the value of 210/106 was obtained, the patient lay prone again. Within five minutes, the B.P. has risen to 218/112. That evening it was 190/90. It appears that the fall in B.P. thruout the day might be due to change in posture. The most likely explanation that occurs to me is that a certain amount of pooling of blood occurs in the abdomen and lower extremities when the patient is upright. When he lies down, the blood volume in the arterial tree is probably greatly increased with the consequent rise in B.P. The question of diminution of the percentage of serum protein with resultant increase in blood volume may also be a factor. Potassium iodide was stopped because of increased nasal congestion. Thesodate, grs. 3–3¼ with Phenobarbital, gr. ¼ t.i.d. given.

4-21-44 Pt. feels very well. No complaints. Ht.—As before. Lungs—A few moist rales heard at both bases. E.K.[G.]—See report. 234/126, 210/114. From the appearance of this E.K.G, it would appear that the digitalis effect is less marked which means that the maintenance dose is not sufficient. Accordingly, an extra tablet (.1 gm.) is to be given today and again Tuesday (4-25-44).

4-23-44 Conference—Admiral McIntire, Captain Harper, Dr. Dickens, Lt. Comdr. Bruenn [Bruenn was in Washington from April 21 to April 27].
1. It was agreed that an increase in the dosage of digitalis was indicated.
2. The program of rest and marked limitation of activity is to be rigidly enforced.
3. Thesodate is to be discontinued, but the Phenobarbital, gr. ¼ is to be continued as a brake on excessive activity as well as a cushion against possible emotional trauma.
4. Dr. Dickens suggested the trial of desiccated thyroid extract, grains ½ each day—to be stepped up to grains 1 each day if necessary. No action on this suggestion was taken.
5. In the vitamin therapy, Multi Cebrin [a multivitamin preparation] was suggested in place of Unicap—because of the former's high B content.
6. The question of abdominal support in the form of an elastic binder, belt or corset was discussed. B.P. 212/114.

4-28-44 Had been asymptomatic until today. Late in the afternoon he began to complain of abdominal pain and tenderness associated with slight nausea. No radiation of the distress. Bowels have been regular. No cardiac symptoms. P.E.—Pulse 76/min. B.P. 230/120. Temp. 98°. H[ear]t and lungs as before. Abdomen was not distended. There was tenderness and voluntary spasm over the R.U.Q., [right upper quadrant of abdomen—liver, gallbladder], the lower RQ [right lower quadrant of abdomen—appendix] and in the epigastrium. Percussion note was tympanitic over the latter but not over the former areas.[5]

4-29-44 Abdominal symptoms persist, practically unchanged. They are apparently not severe enough to interfere with sleep or with appetite. Very loose movements today with much gas. P.E.—Unchanged. The abdominal tenderness however seems less pronounced on palpation. E.K.[G.]—See report. T.P.R. [temperature, pulse, respiration]—normal. Thesodate discontinued. 196/112

4-30-44 Still complains of his abdomen. Bowels very loose (2 movements). No cardiac symptoms. P.E.—Unchanged. T.P.R.—normal. 206/104, 234/120. Placed on a very soft diet, i.e. milk toast, rice pudding, custards.

5-1-44 Free of all abdominal distress. Feels very well, subjectively and objectively is in grand shape. 210/106, 220/116.

5-2-44 Because of his apparent recovery, was placed on a regular diet. Following luncheon, had a recurrence of his abdominal distress, and this evening was acutely uncomfortable. With the use of local applications of heat, and pectin, he was made more comfortable and was able to have a fairly restful night. B.P. 240/130 recorded this evening. Complained of soreness up the back of the neck, and a throbbing sensation all thru the body. No cardiac symptoms.

5-3-44 Abdomen still rather tender to palpation, particularly the R.U.Q. and over the caecum. Soft bland diet resorted to. Has been having two very loose bowel movements in the mornings. No cardiac symptoms. Stayed in bed all day today.

5-4-44 Definitely better. It is notable that during this whole period pt. has been able to eat with apparent appetite altho he tends to belittle it. P.E. Looks very well. Lungs—Entirely clear. H[ear]t.—As before. Apical impulse is in anterior axillary line. First sound at the apex is of relatively good tone and is followed by a soft systolic murmur. $A_2>P_2$ [second heart sound over the aortic-valve area is louder than the second sound over the pulmonic-valve area]. Abdomen—Some residual soreness and tenderness over the R.U.Q. and caecum.

5-5-44 Appears very well. No complaints. In excellent spirits. P.E.—Unchanged. E.K.G.—See report.

5-26-44 X-ray of gall bladder. The gall bladder shows a good functional response. There are indications of a group of cholesterol stones. Because of this report, pt. was placed on a low fat regime—with calories to 1800—for prevention of symptoms as well as to reduce weight. Now weighs about 188.

Blood pressure readings taken twice daily between April 9 and the end of the Hobcaw visit, through June 14, averaged 196/112 on awakening and 194/96 in the evening.[6]

Daisy came down for a few days toward the end of the stay, and first of all noticed the "wonderful bed," this after the usual experience with wartime train travel in which all the sleepers were chock-full and food service was indifferent. Upon arrival she was delighted to see the president, as he was to see her. She noticed that the company at dinner that night, a small group, sat around the table for two hours and then went into the living room. The president talked to Dr. Bruenn, Adm. William D. Leahy (his military chief of staff), and Daisy for a little while and went to bed. She went upstairs to her room. The others settled down to gin rummy, but adjourned at half past ten. "One couldn't imagine a more quiet orderly household."[7]

Daisy arrived on May 4, and her cousin still felt good-for-nothing, but this might have been because of the diet, also because, she wrote, of some sort of an attack that centered in the upper part of the abdomen.

The day after Daisy arrived she learned two things about her cousin's health that are worth mentioning. The one is of interest because Roosevelt never mentioned it to Dr. Bruenn, although it would have been of more than casual concern to the latter. The cardiologist could not get over the fact that the president never gave any indication that he, FDR, knew Bruenn was a cardiologist. Nearly half a century later this strange omission remained in his mind. Upon Daisy's arrival at Hobcaw the president gave her two incomplete letters he had written her, which he planned to send and did not. Undated, they were, Daisy thought, in "an alarmingly shaky hand." In one, the second, he wrote, "I forgot to tell you that Dr. Bruin [sic] came down, too—He is one of the best heart men." So he did, after all, know who Bruenn was.[8]

How this knowledge came is difficult to say. When he went to Bethesda on March 28 he had been wheeled into the Electrocardiograph Department. When Bruenn reappeared at the White House to give him daily medicines the president knew he was a cardiology patient. In bringing in Bruenn on a near daily basis, four days a week or more, McIntire must have talked to Roosevelt and would have had to offer a reason for Bruenn's appearance. The admiral might have mentioned his own responsibilities as surgeon general, but such an explanation would not have sufficed, nor would FDR have allowed it to. The cat would have come out of the bag. The accolade of "one of the best heart men" must have been McIntire's. That Roosevelt never admitted this knowledge to Bruenn, with whom his relations were excellent, was another matter, to be considered later.

The other revelation from the president to his cousin appeared casually in Daisy's diary for May 5. It was a considerable confession from FDR. "From a later talk with the P. the trouble is evidently with the heart," she wrote, "—the diastole & systole are not working properly in unison . . ." Roosevelt thus knew what his trouble was. As Daisy related, "He said he discovered that the doctors had not agreed together about what to tell him, so that he found out that they were not telling *him* the *whole* truth & that he was evidently more sick than they said!"

This information, too, like knowledge of who Bruenn was, the president carefully kept from his cardiologist. Years later Bruenn wondered why FDR never asked about blood pressure readings. The present writer asked Bruenn if he ever had a patient who did not ask about pressures. The answer was, with a grin, "One or two." Here again the Suckley diary, published the year of Bruenn's death, shows why there were no inquiries. The truth was that the president's physical therapist, Fox, was taking blood pressures. The diary makes that point in several entries for December 1944 and January 1945. On January 12, 1945, Fox took the pressures, and Daisy and the president debated the outcome: "today was a record 'low': 190/88. F thinks I am wrong about the 88, that it was 98, but I think I am right—I will ask Fox."[9] Like the president's secretive behavior over the question of whether Bruenn was a cardiologist, so this resort to private blood pressure readings, rather than simply inquiring of his cardiologist, must be considered later.

After the president returned to Washington from Hobcaw the leisurely schedule that marked the weeks in South Carolina was instituted at the White House. The consultants, Lahey and Paullin, advised less activity. Paullin stressed moderation and said the president had driven his automobile tires hard but said they would go another ten thousand miles if he would not take the rough places in the road at too high a speed; it was necessary to reduce to twenty-five or thirty-five miles per hour, then the established speed for driving of cars and conservation of tires during the war. McIntire prescribed ten hours of sleep per night and two rest periods daily totaling nearly three hours between lunch and dinner. The postwar Roosevelt critic John T. Flynn in *The Roosevelt Myth* would point out that the new routine allowed four hours of work a day. Daisy, of course, had noticed this on April 2, before the Hobcaw visit. Hassett defined work as two hours for appointments—11:00 a.m. to 1:00 p.m.—and two after lunch for paperwork, reading letters and memos, and dictating and signing. The president said about this time that during the daily four hours of work in South Carolina the country "got along" and presumably could do the same thereafter.[10]

The president returned from Hobcaw on Sunday, May 7. Thursday, May 11, he and Anna left at half past four for a long weekend at Shangri-La, the retreat in the Catoctin Mountains near Thurmont, Maryland, later known as Camp David (after President Eisenhower's father and grandson). For the weekend he planned almost complete relaxation. Grace Tully was to go up on Friday morning but return that afternoon. On the Thursday of departure the president had two or three visitors, took a nap after lunch, and signed mail.

The new schedule was announced to the nation by the president's wife in her newspaper column, "My Day." Her explanation was approximate as to what was going on. "My great excitement," she wrote for publication on May 11, "was finding the President home. He looks so well that all of us have decided we are going to keep him away from work for certain periods of time, no matter how unpopular we are, because when he is not tired he gives everybody in the house such a tremendous impetus to do more work and take more interest in whatever they are doing."[11]

Over the next weeks Roosevelt continued the schedule. Whether it was effective is difficult to say. He assuredly was not doing much work. If one grouped his four-hour schedule with the fact that he was so often absent from the White House—175 days during the year 1944, the critic Flynn wrote, nine weeks out of the first five months in that year as two other writers have observed—it is clear that during his last year in office he worked a good deal less than four hours a day, perhaps something approaching one or two hours.[12]

The reduction in work hours did not allay the president's concern for his health. After a press conference on May 16 he spoke to one of his staff assistants, Jonathan Daniels, son of former secretary of the navy Josephus Daniels. The younger Daniels looked much like his father, average height, balding. He was a considerable writer of books. The conversation was about a book by the writer George Fort Milton that dealt with presidential power and touched on the lend-lease arrangements with the Soviet Union. Apparently sensitive to what history would say about the Roosevelt administration, perhaps looking otherwise to the future, the president said strangely, "Here is something you ought to write if I should pop off."[13]

There were no other such testimonies. Daisy continued to worry. When "F" went up to Hyde Park for weekends she saw him getting rested on the first day or two, after relaxation returning for three or four days in Washington, getting keyed up, overtired, and repeating the whole process. Late in June he decided to stop cocktails before dinnertime and take sherry instead. Daisy was irritated: "Everyone with high blood pressure I ever heard of has always been deprived of *all* stimulants." The president's color was pretty good when he was not tired. "It is the heart, I suppose, which can go just so long without a rest."[14]

During these weeks nothing seemed to work very well. Daisy wrote on May 22, "He has intentionally been alone this week, without even GGT, & I think it is giving him a little time to think." After two days of quiet she found that he seemed better, "more rested, and as a result, with more energy & ambition to accomplish things." Next day, writing from the third-floor Blue Room in the White House, she remarked the greeting the president received upon coming back to Washington. "As usual, Anna & little Johnny were at the door to greet 'Papa.' Mrs. R. is somewhere in transit & will spend the week-end at H.P." A few days later Daisy and the president were at Shangri-La. "The P. said he had a good night, but he looked tired & drawn, to me. We had a good lunch, with a salad followed by cheese. . . . After lunch, the 'siesta' until 5 mins of 4, & at 4 we started out for a drive of 3 hours in the open car." Next day, back in Washington, it was a matter of dodging a women's group that the president's wife had brought in for lunch. "We lunched on the porch, on the side away from the rose garden, as Mrs. R. was having a 'small lunch' of 50 ladies on the lawn. The ladies were kept in the Red Room until the P. came in & went up in the elevator. Then the ladies were loosened onto the lawn & the P. went to his peaceful lunch with Anna & me. After lunch he rested for an hour." On May 31 everything worked out all right, a "busy routine day," with the "P." beginning appointments at half past eleven, taking his rest and massage, and swimming for the first time in months. He found his lower weight, 178, made everything easier, such as walking in the water. June 1, Daisy recorded, "Mrs. R. blew in from N.Y. for a moment & blew out again to get ready for some woman of the Press she was entertaining at 9."[15]

While these events were transpiring, with the president doing all right but not notably better, Daisy tried to believe that the president was taking Mlle Gassette's salts. She had given them and the necessary instructions to Anna to give to the doctors. It was possible, she thought, that the instructions challenged the doctors and although the presidential physicians naturally discredited the pills they really were using them, for the president was taking two pills after each meal and one contained vitamins. (The other doubtless was digitalis.) Daisy also noticed a "rather extraordinary thing" in treatment of the president. This was that FDR had not had his sinus treatment even once "as far as I can find out!!"

In regard to the sinus treatments, it should be said that neither McIntire nor, as sometimes seems to have been the case, Commander Fox was doing them on a regular basis. Daisy did not understand that most of the time Dr. Robert T. Canon, an excellent practitioner, head of the department at Bethesda, was handling sinus problems. He treated FDR's nose with Argyrol. A silver-based antibacterial, it was a simple and effective packing. He would pack the president's nose and place him under a heat lamp, then remove the packs and suction the nostrils clean. Dr. Canon visited the president frequently, as often as twice a day. Years later a story circulated that navy physicians used an adrenalin spray, which would have elevated the president's blood pressure. Another story had it that the navy physicians thoughtfully packed the presidential nose with cocaine.[16]

By early July the problem of the moment, which the president had to confront for more reasons than he may have understood, was the need to choose a running mate for the fourth term.

On this score, as on others, FDR received no help from his wife. A dozen years later when President Eisenhower in 1956 decided to run for a second term after his heart attack, reporters asked the former president's widow about her husband's decision in 1944, and Mrs. Roosevelt made everything clear. She said her husband's doctors found him "well and active" and he needed only to "rest every day" to ease a heart weakened by the strain of the war years. They told him he "could quite easily go on with the activities of the presidency." She said, "He never gave his health much thought and neither did any of us." She disclosed that there never had been any family discussion, even between the president and her, about a fourth term. "I wouldn't discuss it with him because I hated the idea and he knew I hated it. Either he felt he ought to serve a fourth term and wanted it or he didn't. That was up to the man himself to decide and no one else."[17]

That he should not have run again in 1944 should have gone without saying. Years later Anna's husband, Dr. Halsted, reviewing the evidence, related that "on medical grounds alone, he should not have run in 1944." When Dr. Bruenn himself looked back on the issue many years later, he avowed that although no one ever asked him about the fourth term, if anyone had inquired of him he would have said it was impossible medically.[18]

People around the president believed Roosevelt wanted to run. The head of the White House Secret Service detail, Michael F. Reilly, who saw a great deal of "the Boss," thought Roosevelt had two reasons for running.[19] One was the war. The other was that FDR felt he would make a better commander in chief than anyone else. The latter may have been the nub of the issue. The president enjoyed the White House for the power it gave him. He may have given the impression that he was tiring of the rigmarole, the ceremonial, but one suspects he enjoyed that too. The White House provided the ultimate in personal convenience. Whatever the convenience of Hyde Park, the White House was more so, with everything provided for.

Moreover, whatever the president's illness the Democratic Party needed him in 1944, for Dewey seemed a serious candidate, especially because of his relative youth—he was forty-two compared to Roosevelt's sixty-two. Wendell Willkie in 1940 had scared Roosevelt, for he appeared formidable. For a while in 1944, Dewey looked the same way. Certainly the party bosses felt that the president needed to run. Early in 1944 the former chairman of the national committee, Postmaster Gen. Frank C. Walker, was asked to go over to the Mayflower Hotel and see his predecessor as chairman, the boss of the Bronx, Flynn, who had just seen the president and was beside himself with fear that Roosevelt would not run. For a while in the late winter and early spring the president spoke that way. Walker may have sought to allay Flynn's concern, for already the president had spoken otherwise—he had expressed interest in a fourth term to Walker in 1942. Roosevelt had talked both ways in 1939–1940 and taken the nomination after encouraging others to do so. He was to do the same thing in 1944, although less so; he wobbled but this time did not suggest others.

What was a quiet, conspiratorial issue in early 1944 was that several leading Democratic politicos observed how ill Roosevelt appeared, without knowing the cause, for they had heard the rumors, and decided among themselves that Vice President Wallace would not do in terms of renomination—there was danger that whoever obtained the vice presidency would become president. The leader of the conspiracy was the party treasurer, Edwin W. Pauley, who got together with the president's appointments secretary, Pa Watson, and the two brought in Flynn and Walker and their successor as party chairman, Robert E. Hannegan, formerly commissioner of internal revenue, together with Mayor Edward J. Kelly of Chicago who was to be host to the national convention in mid-July. Through Watson they saw to it that delegates to the forthcoming convention who were anti-Wallace were admitted to the president's office where they would divulge their sentiments. Wallace supporters found presidential appointments difficult, perhaps impossible. Gradually the anti-Wallace visitors turned the president against the then vice president.[20]

A possible substitution for Wallace at Chicago was the president's "assistant president," the principal White House assistant, former senator from South Carolina and for a year associate justice of the Supreme Court. James F. Byrnes wanted the nomination for the same reason Wallace did: Roosevelt's ill health. The president disliked Byrnes, who was useful as an assistant but "pushy" in the White House, where he constantly was threatening to resign. Byrnes appeared too interested in his own advancement.

At the convention the finger of destiny pointed to Senator Truman, but not before the choosing of a running mate became a most awkward problem. The leaders could not talk it over with the president, and the latter wobbled far too long, coming out in favor of Truman during a White House summit meeting on the evening of July 11, eight days before the convention opened in Chicago, but telling Wallace that if he, FDR, were a delegate to the convention (he was not going to be) he would vote for Wallace, and telling Byrnes that the South Carolinian was his choice. He seemed to opt for Byrnes when his train passed through Chicago on Saturday, July 15, en route to San Diego where he would board a heavy cruiser for a trip to Hawaii. He told Hannegan, with whom he spoke in Chicago, that he favored Byrnes. Monday night, July 17, from his train, the president finished off Byrnes by telling the leaders in Chicago to go "all out" for Truman. Byrnes withdrew, but without direct word from the president Wallace refused, and on the following Thursday night his supporters crowded into the balconies and onto the floor of Chicago Stadium and nearly stampeded the convention. The leaders declared the crowded hall a fire hazard and adjourned the session until the next day, turning out the lights on the platform and podium. The tactic gave them time to convert the delegates to what the president wanted.

The choosing of Truman on July 21, 1944, was a very close call, and one suspects the president nearly lost control because of inability to focus on the problem and at crucial moments make up his mind. Wednesday evening, the night after the White House meeting that chose Truman, the president called Daisy about the problem. "He confessed to an exhausting week, & that he must keep going for another 24 hrs. His voice sounded tired & he was working on the V.P. problem. That meant talking, discussing, trying to find compromises between disagreeing parties, etc.—In a word, thoroughly harassing & wearing . . ."[21]

The president gave his acceptance speech from San Diego, and the photographs taken of the affair, his sitting behind a table aboard the presidential train with a few people along the windows were terrible. The small table revealed the president's thin, withered legs, and the wide trousers of the time accentuated them. He was reading the address, and his face was turned down, hence elongated, which made him look unwell. He had his mouth open, the photographs caught him speaking, which gave the appearance of an inability to control his facial muscles and perhaps having suffered some sort of stroke.

The photograph problem during the acceptance speech much bothered Press Secretary Early, who wrote Grace Tully about it:

> I was terrifically disappointed, let down to a new low, when I saw the photograph of the President delivering his speech of acceptance. I can't imagine what was wrong with Skadding, or his camera, or his subject. But something decidedly was wrong. I have not seen the newsreels. I hope they are better than the stills. Upon inquiry, the newsreel editors in New York tell me that the motion pictures are "fairly good." I also hear that the President ate something on the train which upset his stomach and that his appearance was not good the night he spoke. In fact, I understand that Hugo Johnson spoke to Ross McIntire and suggested that the pictures be postponed until the following morning—until the President had had a good night's sleep. The rumor factory is working overtime—making all it can out of rumors and lies about the President's health. That is why some of the photographs I have seen caused me much concern at this time.[22]

The photographer, George Skadding, found himself on the carpet with the irascible Early, and offered his own explanation:

> When I brought the pictures in from San Diego it was extremely late—the A.P., Acme and INP were holding their wires open overtime. I turned the negatives over to them to rush through, and due to the close deadline they were working on, they grabbed the first shot they looked at and before I knew it they had this particular bad shot on the wires. I did get them to transmit a good close up later, hoping it would kill the first one. There were several other shots that could have been used.[23]

While the train was at San Diego the president's son James, a big, husky marine colonel, attended his father, and in a later book related a story about his father undergoing a heart attack or stroke, during which "Jimmy" lifted him to the floor and allowed him to lie there. "Jimmy, I don't know if I can make it," the president allegedly said. "I have horrible pains." Jimmy gripped his hand and said he would call the doctor. His father said no, it was stomach pains from eating too quickly. It was not his heart, he said. Jimmy wrote that he could do nothing else but let his father lie there, "He was not only my father, he was the commander in chief." At last the president, according to the story, opened his eyes, color returned to his face, and breathing was easier. "Help me up now, Jimmy," he said.[24]

James Roosevelt told this story in books published in 1959 and 1976, and his sister, Anna, believed the episode either did not happen or, if it did, Jimmy had been completely irresponsible, for it would have been his duty to report it to Dr. Bruenn who was aboard the train. If it did happen, one must presume it was another gallbladder attack.

The president thereupon boarded the cruiser *Baltimore*, bound for Hawaii, and throughout the voyage rested in the admiral's cabin. During the trip Bruenn wrote in his diary that the president was fine.[25]

Then came the reception at Pearl Harbor, July 26:

> Raised Molokai on the port side about 11 a.m. A beautiful day. About 12, raised Diamond Head and Koko Head. At 2 could easily see Oahu. A beautiful island with large green mountains, with their crests [peaks] covered with clouds. Houses clinging to sides. President came up to flag deck about this time. Talked about the Pali and Kamehameha. Just outside Pearl Harbor met by an Admiral's barge. Admirals Nimitz and Ghormley came aboard. Entrance into Pearl Harbor—what a sight. Hundreds of ships from air carriers, battleships, cruisers to tugs—all with their crews in white "manning the rail." Bands playing. Men at attention. Our vessel moved slowly up the channel, bugle playing at intervals. The most impressive sight I have *ever* witnessed.[26]

The *Baltimore* was a great new ship, 14,500 tons, nearly seven hundred feet long, narrow, with beautiful lines, bristling with guns. As the reception at Pearl Harbor revealed that wartime security had been broken (the president's visit was known for two days beforehand), the cruiser's captain made the most of it, hoisting the presidential flag at the main—a glorious ensign, a great eagle on a field of blue, with stars in each corner. At dockside the pier was packed, and the admirals and generals came aboard. Bruenn was astonished, twenty-two of the former and eighteen of the latter.

After the reception it was off to "the Holmes place" where the president was to stay. The house was at Waikiki, five minutes from the Royal Hawaiian; both used the same beach. And "what a place!!" It was a large house, three stories. The entire street was blocked off with double lines of barricades, marines on duty outside the high walls along the beach, ships patrolling the sea. The house had gardens in front, a large ground floor tremendous in area, with heightened bedrooms. The second floor was a lanai, stairs outside, open on three sides, filled with couches. The top floor was the president's suite, two tremendous rooms, Bruenn wrote, with three exposures. Behind the house was a terrace with palm trees in front of the beach, large cushioned easy chairs arranged in likely places, cottages on the side. Bruenn upon espying the water went in almost immediately, found the experience unbelievable, warm yet invigorating, clean, the surf most enjoyable.

Arrival in Pearl Harbor, the drive to Honolulu, the Holmes house, and swimming preceded cocktails and dinner with the president. Afterward Bruenn went out with Judge Rosenman and a friend to see the town after ten o'clock that night. There was a curfew, and the town was deserted. He enjoyed a chocolate soda in a place where he was served by Japanese American waitresses.

Next day, July 27, they went to Schofield Barracks for a review, and to Wheeler Field for another. At dinner that night were Gen. Douglas MacArthur, Adm. William F. Halsey, and Adm. Chester W. Nimitz.

On the morning of July 28 the conference on Pacific strategy took place between the president, Nimitz, MacArthur, and Admiral Leahy. There was only a single session, lasting two hours and a half, an absurd amount of time for deciding so important a matter. After the conference pictures were taken.

The president's party left Hawaii on the twenty-ninth after a visit to Hickam Field where Bruenn saw "planes and planes," with the field's personnel all lined up and at attention. Thence to the navy yard: "Battleships, the sub base, torpedo shops, biggest yard in the world." Lunch was served at Nimitz's quarters; all those present were admirals and generals except three captains and Bruenn.. After lunch Roosevelt visited a five-hundred-bed hospital. Then a press conference, and the *Baltimore* took on the presidential group and moved slowly through the base and out again to sea.

The first two days after Oahu, en route to the Aleutians, were warm and sunny, after which the fog closed in, almost constant until arrival two days later at Adak. Bruenn, a landlubber, found the voyage "rather boring and after a few days of it enough." Twenty-six hundred men and eight women, nurses, at Adak and "No venereal disease!" He remarked the dreariness of the whole place. The ship was unable to leave because of a crosswind, despite the efforts of five tugs, and the party spent another twenty-four hours at the mooring.

Then it was Kodiak Island on August 7. The party reviewed the naval air station and army troops, dust everywhere, then drove through the village, fished six miles inland at a lovely little lake and stream where the president caught a single fish, a brook trout, and transferred to the destroyer *Cummings* for transit of the inside passage through the Panhandle to Bremerton. August 22, Bruenn wrote of having "just returned from a 6 weeks' inspection tour of Hawaii and the Aleutian Islands. Trip was characterized by rather strenuous schedules while ashore which the patient performed without apparent undue fatigue."

It was the stopover in Bremerton that led to a nearly embarrassing and in its private particulars dangerous attack of angina, in the midst of the president's speech before thirty thousand people and a national radio audience. The speech was a poor production, written without benefit of either Grace Tully, who would not have hesitated to correct it, or the president's principal speechwriters, Sam Rosenman and the playwright Robert E. Sherwood. Roosevelt dictated it to Lt. William M. Rigdon, the naval stenographer on shipboard. The president knew it was not one of his better efforts and envisioned it as not too important—it was "a homey report" on the trip and hence allowable. Tully thought it "one of the poorest speeches he ever made, both in form and in delivery."[27]

Tully was present at Bremerton when the president gave the speech standing—he was in his braces, the first time in months—on the forecastle of the *Cummings*. The braces did not fit, for he had lost weight because of the diet. The crowd was unresponsive; it comprised people who had just gotten off work at the navy yard, and the president did not make an entrance, which would have produced cheering, but sat on the deck for fifteen minutes before speaking. The speech was too long, thirty-five minutes, and was dull and wandering.

But most important was the chest pain that radiated to both shoulders. It lasted fifteen minutes, gradually subsiding. When he finished and had left the forecastle, he said to Bruenn, "I had a severe pain!" The physician and his assistants stripped him down in the cabin and took some blood and made a cardiogram. Fortunately it was angina, not a heart attack. Yet it pointed out something that Bruenn hitherto had not been, could not have been, certain of. The president always had denied pain. It was the first observation that Bruenn had made: "This was proof positive that he had coronary disease, no question about it."[28]

In the book published in 1946, Admiral McIntire wrote that a stiff wind was blowing and there was a slant to the deck, which forced the president to brace himself. As a result Roosevelt finished up with considerable pain. "Purely muscular, as it turned out; and when we got back to Washington on August 17, after journeying 13,912 miles, he was in better shape than when he left."[29]

2

In the months between the president's return from Hawaii on August 12 and the end of 1944 events cascaded, as one would have expected. Always something was going on, and both to the president and to his countrymen the appearance of things was of incessant activity. In actual fact matters were not so active. Behind the facade of movement, of decisions, of control from the executive offices to the rear of the White House, there often was little but emptiness, with the government virtually running itself. As had been happening for months prior to the Hawaii trip, the same was true thereafter: the president frequently was not in the mansion. He was at Hyde Park or Shangri-La or Warm Springs. There he could manage the quiet days that Daisy Suckley so often saw, one following the other, in which he remained in bed until close to lunchtime and then proceeded according to the routine established after his return from South

Carolina. When at the Hudson valley estate or up in the Catoctin Mountains or at the cottage in Warm Springs he had few, frequently no, visitors and thus saved the energy he lost in seeing people, the diminishment that conversation and attention inevitably charged upon his energies.

There were a few interruptions. On September 12–16 he was in Quebec attending a conference with Churchill and the prime minister of Canada, W. L. Mackenzie King. The latter worried about the president's appearance. "It seemed to me," he wrote in his diary, " . . . that he had failed very much since I last saw him. He is very much thinner in body and also is much thinner in his face. He looks distinctly older and worn. I confess I was just a little shocked at his appearance." He asked the president's naval aide, Vice Adm. Wilson Brown, about him, and Brown said the president was seeking to reduce his weight, which gave him that appearance. He added that the president's physician, McIntire, was "really concerned about him," that he did not sit out in the sun, did not get the rest he needed.

The Canadian prime minister worried about the president's judgment. At a luncheon Churchill leaned over and reminded the president that it was necessary to make a toast to the king. Roosevelt did so, but did it in a rambling manner. He made the whole thing too personal. He referred to a great gentleman who had visited him and his wife at Washington and Hyde Park, to other close friends including the governor general of Canada and his wife (the Earl of Athlone and Princess Alice), and said Churchill was a great friend. "There was the closest friendship with everyone—the same for the king, the same for the Athlones, the same for Churchill, etc."[30] It was an interesting slipup, a sign that the president might be acquiring regal qualities from associating with too many regal personalities. Mackenzie King was a shrewd observer. He was an evangelical churchman and critical of people who put on airs. Admittedly he was also an odd duck. He was a spiritualist, full of wisdom about signs and omens that fortunately he confided to his voluminous diary. Still, he had seen something during the Quebec Conference. He had seen the president lose his usual sense of appropriateness, perhaps let down his guard.

On the evening of September 15 the conferees watched a new movie about Woodrow Wilson. It was a color film, and the sets looked much like the White House. The actor playing Wilson was Alexander Knox, whose film credits consisted entirely of the Wilson role in which he was stunningly convincing. The point of the film was that the president during World War I, whom Roosevelt as a young man often had seen, fought so hard for the future of America and the world, pinning his hopes on the League of Nations, that his health gave way, collapsed, with the stroke of October 2, 1919. During the showing Dr. Bruenn sat near the president and heard him mutter, as if to no one, "By God, that's not going to happen to me!"[31]

At the conference Roosevelt's blood pressures were high, as high as 240/130. The latter reading occurred the night of the Wilson movie, after which the president got to bed at two o'clock in the morning.[32]

Near the end of the conference, just before the president's train left Quebec, Churchill asked Admiral McIntire, who was present, to come to his room. The prime minister desired a confidential statement concerning the president's condition. He had been alarmed by reports. McIntire gave him what the physician described as "the results of our June checkup," by which he may have meant the checkup for the gallbladder attacks after the month in South Carolina—there is no record of a checkup in June 1944. There was nothing organically wrong, he said, although he stressed the president's age and the strain of nearly twelve years. If Roosevelt did not overdo, there was every reason to believe he could "win through." The prime minister doubtless had readied a statement for whatever intelligence he was to receive. It was Churchillian. "With all my heart I hope so," he responded. "We cannot have anything happen to this man. His usefulness to the world is paramount during these troubled times."[33]

After the president got back home and took up his routine, things seemed to go along all right. No harm had been done at Quebec. No word of his condition had gotten out there. Mackenzie King thought he observed a decline, but only told his diary about it; Churchill tried to get information from McIntire but failed. Bruenn found the situation about the same on September 20:

> No cardiac symptoms. Patient has been standardized on .1 gm.
> of digitalis q.D. [daily] with an extra dose (.1 gm.) twice a
> week. Appetite is rather . . . [unreadable] but complains of no
> abdominal discomfort. Still insistent in his desire to lose more
> weight—but this must be guarded against. He has already lost

more weight than is deemed wise. Calories in diet to be increased
and increase in weight is to be encouraged. Now weighs 168.
It has been noted that the blood pressure levels during the
past few weeks have been somewhat higher than previously,
with however return to more usual levels when relaxed and
at ease. . . . Phenobarbital increased from ¼ grain to ½ grain.
P.E.—Unchanged—the blood pressure has ranged from 180/100
to 240/130.

In the facade of activity that managed to shield the president's
inactivity there was one threatened breach of security, one might
describe it, and this was the talk of Roosevelt's illness that began to
circulate among physicians both at Bethesda and at the Mayo Clinic.
Fortunately a quick investigation by the FBI seems to have put an
end to the loose remarks. But the remarks were not so loose, for they
were based on solid information.[34]

It is unclear whether the talk arose because of the chance photographing of Dr. Bruenn with the president, in the Skadding photograph showing Roosevelt giving his acceptance speech aboard his
train at San Diego, or whether it was out of the normal conversation
among physicians at Bethesda, as would have happened at any hospital, military or civil. It perhaps arose because of both. When Roosevelt gave the acceptance speech the doctors at Bethesda of course
recognized Bruenn in the photograph, and that raised the possibility
that the president was suffering from cardiovascular disease. Several
months earlier Bruenn suddenly and inexplicably had left his post at
Bethesda. Dr. Ross Golden at Columbia Presbyterian saw the photograph in the July 31 issue of *Life* magazine and during a meeting at
the Palmer House in Chicago of the Board of Examiners of Radiology,
a medical group that certified radiologists, told an X-ray specialist
attached to the army surgeon general's office, Col. Byrl R. Kirklin, he
had seen Bruenn. "Did you notice the unidentified profile in the picture to the right of the President?" he asked. "That man is Dr. Bruenn,
a cardiologist at the Presbyterian Hospital in New York City."

Then there was conversation between physicians, and Dr. Kirklin
heard it. He traveled between Washington and the Mayo Clinic
in Rochester, Minnesota, where he instructed army corpsmen in
X-ray techniques. He attended a luncheon at the Kahler Hotel in
Rochester in company with other physicians, including the head of

the diagnostic section at the clinic, Dr. A. R. Barnes. The latter had recently returned from Bethesda where there had been a meeting of heart specialists, and during the luncheon Barnes said the president had a serious heart ailment. Later that day, October 21, Kirklin participated in a poker game and among those present were several more doctors, and Kirklin quoted the remark of Barnes.

The word obviously was out about what was the trouble with the president, and the statements by Colonel Kirklin reached the ears of Asst. Secy. of State Breckinridge Long, who sent a letter to the president's press secretary, Steve Early. The latter called the office of Dir. J. Edgar Hoover of the FBI and spoke with Hoover's second-in-command, E. A. Tamm, who sensed that the problem was a little politically tinged and said the military services should police their own members. Perhaps with support of McIntire or the president himself, Early then wrote a memorandum to Hoover, who chose to ignore the legal question raised by Tamm and told his assistant to go into action, and Tamm's agents turned up the names of Drs. Golden and Barnes and those of half a dozen other physicians at Bethesda and the Mayo Clinic.

According to the resultant FBI report, dated October 29, which was three days after the initial letter from Long to Early identifying Colonel Kirklin, the FBI agents were especially hard on a young physician at Bethesda, a navy lieutenant, Dr. Howard Odel, first interviewed at Bethesda on October 27. Odel was a close friend of Dr. Barnes and a former protégé of his at the Mayo Clinic. Barnes had told the FBI that Odel made a statement to him when the two were walking about the grounds at Bethesda on October 19, that "The President is a very sick man—heart disease." Confronted with this information, Odel denied any such statement but said the president's health had been the subject of a general discussion at a recent luncheon at Bethesda. He declined to name the attendees at the luncheon. He was "obviously disturbed and uneasy" during his interview. The FBI came back the next day, and after more questioning he was confronted with the fact that it was Dr. Barnes who had said he, Odel, was talking about the president. Odel explained that he had shown Dr. Barnes through the hospital and that rumors were circulating about the president's health and he, Odel, wondered aloud if the president had heart disease or hypertension. He told

Barnes that the president had been at Bethesda on two or three occasions and for that reason he wondered if something was wrong with the president's heart. He advised the FBI that he may have said, "I suspect there may be something to it." He had not made a flat statement that the president was a very sick man. He realized his statement to Barnes had been very imprudent, but had worked for Barnes for twelve years and knew of his interest in heart disease because Barnes was an eminent heart specialist. He said that another Mayo physician, a Dr. Feldman, recently had been at Bethesda and asked Odel if he knew anything about the president's health, and Odel replied that he did not, taking this position because he did not feel he knew Feldman well enough to talk to him. One can guess that after such grilling at Bethesda and the Mayo Clinic there was little more talk.

In any event, by the time of the FBI report, the end of October, attention throughout the country had turned—in addition to constant reports about the war in Europe and the Far East—to the presidential election, and something needs be said about the president's activities in that regard. After returning from Hawaii, Roosevelt had met with his running mate, of whom he had seen little. He had not seen Senator Truman since March 5. It was not merely important but necessary to show friendship to the man who, unknown to the president, would succeed him. At the moment the necessity also was to show solidarity on the ticket, the two leaders moving forward to advance the nation's purposes, united in the struggle against reaction personified by Governor Dewey.

The meeting took place in the form of a luncheon at a table set up behind the White House under a magnolia tree (planted by Andrew Jackson, or so Truman—ever the historical observer—thought). It was a beautiful day, August 18, 1944, and the two candidates sat close together behind the table, photographers swarming in front of them. The photographer for *Life*, George Tames, took a fine picture that day, the candidates looking at him, Truman grinning attractively, a striped tie fronting his striped shirt, thick glasses not shining (Tames was too good a photographer for that). The president held his pince-nez and looked across the table with a pleasant half smile. The handsome face of the country's leader since 1933 looked better than it had appeared elsewhere that year—Roosevelt showed no real change since earlier years, for Tames avoided the thinness by photographing him slightly sideways. The president wore a white shirt on which his nattily tied polka-dot bow tie stood out beautifully. On the lower left-hand sleeve of his shirt was stitched a set of initials turned slightly upward, "F.D.R."[35]

The vice presidential candidate wrote his wife, Bess, afterward about his reception, how he had entered the White House at about five minutes to one—when great events happen people always remember details. The president was nice as he could be, and the senator wrote, "You'd have thought I was the long lost brother or the returned Prodigal." Before going outside Truman told Roosevelt of his appreciation for "putting the finger on me" for vice president, and they talked about the campaign, reconversion after the war, post-war employment, China, the George and Kilgore Bills then before Congress. When luncheon was announced they adjourned to the "back yard" under the Jackson tree, and "the movie men and then the flashlight boys" went to work. The president became hungry, and sent them off, and the president's daughter acted as hostess. The senator wrote that Anna expressed "a lot of regret" that Bess was not present. Truman told the president his wife was in Missouri attending to the senator's business, and the president said that was all right. FDR gave Truman "a lot of hooey" about what he, Truman, could do to assist the campaign. In the course of the conversation Roosevelt told his running mate that his own wife, Eleanor, was a very timid woman and when he first ran for governor of New York she would not go to political meetings nor make any speeches. He added, "Now she talks all the time."[36]

Upon leaving, Truman did not tell the whole truth to reporters waiting at the White House gate. "He's still the leader he's always been," the senator told them, "and don't let anybody kid you about it. He's keen as a briar." In private, upon return to his Senate office, he told his administrative assistant, "You know, I am concerned about the president's health. I had no idea he was in such a feeble condition. In pouring cream in his tea, he got more cream in the saucer than he did in the cup. His hands are shaking and he talks with considerable difficulty. . . . It doesn't seem to be any mental lapse of any kind, but physically he's just going to pieces. I'm very much concerned about him."[37]

During the lunch, or before, presumably not in company of Anna, the president said something to Truman about how the latter should travel during the campaign. The words as Truman remembered them were uncertain, but he told the story to his World War I lieutenant in Battery D of the 129th Field Artillery Regiment, Vic H. Housholder, to his press secretary Charles G. Ross, and repeated it in his memoirs. It was to the effect that when Truman traveled he should not use an airplane, for it was necessary that "you take care of yourself."[38]

In passing, one should remark Senator Truman's concern that Roosevelt's hands were shaking. Dr. Bruenn later said he thought this fact, noted by others, was not of much importance. Tremors were frequent in individuals of Roosevelt's age. Moreover, he, Bruenn, had seen the president eat many times and not spill anything.[39]

It is possible that Truman's explanations of what happened at the luncheon were mistaken, that Roosevelt's successor read the future into the past. Secretary Ickes lunched with the president a month later, perhaps under the same magnolia tree. Anna was present, the three of them sat in the shade, with the sun out, and it was very pleasant without being at all warm. The secretary frequently saw the president and told his diary that Roosevelt was "decidedly" showing the busyness of the last eleven and a half years, his face thinner, the dark patches under his eyes more pronounced than Ickes could remember. But "he seemed keen and alert and unless something should strike him pretty hard I suspect that he is good for four years more."[40]

About the time Ickes lunched with Roosevelt, Truman had another portent of the future. The president was in Washington, and the senator and his World War I army friend Edward D. McKim, an insurance executive in Omaha, attended a tea at the White House for the cast of the movie *Wilson*. This was on September 7. They spent perhaps an hour and a half at the reception, and went out through the entrance in the east wing. As McKim remembered, he stopped in the street and said to the senator, "Hey bud, turn around and take a look. You're going to be living in that house before long." Truman replied, "Eddie, I'm afraid I am." The senator added about the prospect, "And it scares the hell out of me."[41]

One of the outward purposes of putting Truman into the campaign as vice presidential nominee was to send him out on the hustings to speak for the busy, it was said, president. Wallace, of course, could have done equally well, but there was the special problem with his candidacy. In any event, as the Republican candidate, Dewey, began to speak against the president, referring to him and his assistants as a group of "tired old men," it became almost necessary for the president to show himself, to go out to the large cities at least and indicate that although he was the champ, as ever, he was able to engage in the rough-and-tumble of American politics with any opponent the GOP could put up. The last three weekends before the election, therefore, Roosevelt showed himself. The most notable occasion was in New York City, on a windswept, raw Saturday, October 21, when he toured four boroughs and proved he could take it with the best of his opponents. He followed the next Friday with a speech at Shibe Field in Philadelphia, and next day was in Chicago where Mayor Kelly gathered a vast throng of one hundred thousand to shout for the Democratic Party and its perennial leader. The next Saturday, November 4, Roosevelt was in Boston, after which he adjourned to Hyde Park where on the day before the vote he undertook his traditional tour of Dutchess County and then, on the next Tuesday after that month's first Monday, Tuesday the seventh, voted and awaited the verdict, which as even the Republican opposition guessed was not long in coming: another Roosevelt victory.

In the tours of the last weeks the trip to New York stood out, as it appeared to be a triumph, beyond question. The president had left a rain-drenched Washington for an equally wet New York City to let people see him as he looked and judge his physical fitness with their own eyes. He traveled in an open automobile, at times hatless, through Brooklyn, Queens, the Bronx, and Manhattan. Almost from the start of the journey he was soaking wet, and stopped briefly on one occasion to discard a soaked suit, don another, and go on. At Ebbets Field ten thousand Brooklynites saw the big gates in deep center field open to allow passage of the president's automobile, and rose to their feet shouting a welcome: "We Want Roosevelt!" The president made a short speech, relating that New York's Sen. Robert F. Wagner "deserves well of mankind" and should be returned to the Senate. He left his automobile for his remarks and stood hatless before the microphone, facing a lashing rain.

On he went, mile after mile, fifty-one of them, for four hours. It
was raining when he started at the Brooklyn army base of the New
York Port of Embarkation, and still pouring, the wind colder, when
he passed through Times Square and drove down to the Washington
Square apartment of Mrs. Roosevelt, where he rested for his evening
address at the Waldorf-Astoria. For most of the trip his wife "took
it" with the president, sitting beside him and smiling, wearing a
dark red, fur-collared coat and dark felt hat. Estimates of the crowds
varied, with the police department of Mayor Fiorello LaGuardia
loyally estimating three million onlookers, the same as during the
campaign of 1940. Privately, police officials were not so sure, as the
weather drove people indoors—an honest figure might have been
one million. The car passed at twenty to thirty miles an hour. Crowds
waved small American flags. Most onlookers were in Manhattan,
and as the president's entourage reached the garment district the
crowds vastly increased, an estimated thirty-five hundred people to
each block from Forty-second Street to Thirty-fourth. After the rest at
the apartment the president spoke that evening to the Foreign Policy
Association, and by all accounts spoke well, with his accustomed
vigor.

An interesting footnote to the New York trip, and the triumph it
seemed, was the attitude of the president's longtime friend Ed Flynn
toward what had happened. He was, in a word, furious; he thought
the trip most ill-advised. After the war, in preparation for his book,
You're the Boss, Flynn dictated his memories, and on January 29, 1946,
related an off-the-record point to his secretary, Grace C. Harrington:

Q: What about his [FDR's] tours and speaking engagements,
particularly the one to New York during that awful weather?

A: I was so mad about that that I went up to the country and
was not here. I had arranged for him to speak before the Foreign
Policy Association, with the idea that it could be done and he
could go right back. Then they began to urge him to take the trip
around the city. He called me on the telephone and asked me
what to do. I told him to tell them that I had charge of things in
New York, and to refer them to me, and I would tell them all to
go to hell. But he didn't. I bullied them and made them call off a
lot of trips they wanted him to take.

Q: Do you think he would have lived through the campaign if he'd made them?

A: No.[42]

To the surprise of his physicians Roosevelt went through the campaign very well. McIntire wrote in his book that after Quebec he, the president's physician, dreaded the campaign. To this judgment he added hastily, "but the manner in which the President came through it made me doubt my accuracy as a diagnostician." Covering the weeks from September 20 to November 1 he set out the details: "Temperature—98.6—no elevations; general appearance—color good; present weight—172. Lungs clear; heart—no cardiac symptoms at any time—sounds are good in character; pulse rate ranges 68 to 74. Blood pressure of labile type; systolic ranging from 165 to 180; diastolic 88 to 100; electrocardiogram shows no changes from that of May examination . . ."[43] It was a curious appraisal, considering what individuals said who saw the president, considering what King and Churchill and Bruenn had seen during the Quebec Conference. It was another of the reassuring outlooks, part of the confidence building, perhaps; or might it have been McIntire's own confidence building in light of what was to happen? For the president's physician to take such a position seems almost inexplicable. The first pressure Bruenn recorded in his diary after September 20, on November 18, was higher than what McIntire wrote, namely, 210/112. But Bruenn at this time was also fairly optimistic. He wrote on October 29:

> During the past month he has engaged in more than the usual amount of activity (election). This has included a complete disregard of the rest regime together with periods of prolonged exposure (weather) and intervals of rather intense activity. Speeches have been delivered largely while sitting. Despite this, B.P. levels have been, if anything, lower than before. Patient is eating fairly well and he has not contracted any upper respiratory infection. P.E.—Unchanged. Patient appears to be well stabilized on his digitalis regime.

The skeptical historian Dr. Park has asked about McIntire's words set out above, why the presidential physician was dreading the campaign if Roosevelt was the picture of health for a man his age. Specifically, Park wrote, why the dread when nothing serious would have come from sinuses and bronchitis, "no serious source of concern for the successful completion of even the most vigorous of campaigns!"[44]

November 18, Bruenn wrote another of his occasional (at this time) diary comments:

> No cardiac symptoms. Appetite has again become poor, and patient has lost a little more weight. (Blood pressure levels about as before.) Has been taking additional nourishment in the form of eggnogs (1,500 calories). All restrictions have been removed from the diet. P.E. Looks tired. Color fair. Lies flat without dyspnea. Eyes—No significant retinal sclerosis. Lungs—clear. Heart—Apical impulse 3–4 cm. beyond the nipple line. Sounds are clear and of good quality. First sound at apex is followed by a soft systolic murmur. A_2 is greater than P_2. No diastolic murmurs. B.P. 210/112. Abdomen—soft. Liver not palpable.

Not long afterward, November 27, the president left Washington by train for three weeks at Warm Springs. In this relaxed, familiar place, his appetite improved in a small way, but his weight remained unchanged at 165 pounds (McIntire's figure for September–November 1 was 172). At Warm Springs a lower right molar tooth loosened and was painful, and a dentist, Maj. Benjamin Rubin, summoned from a nearby army base, removed it under local anesthesia, without difficulty; Dr. Rubin was allowed to keep the tooth. There were few visitors, and except for handling the contents of the pouch that arrived each day from Washington the president spent his time reading, motoring about the grounds of the Warm Springs Foundation, and in conversation with staff members who had accompanied him or with local friends.

He did not look very well at this time. Daisy went down, and recounted for November 29 that she found herself gazing at him at least half the time she was in his presence. He was pale, thin, and tired. "I try so hard to make myself think he looks well, but he doesn't. His colour at times seems better than it has been, but he gets very grey when tired, and it shows so much when he is sitting under bright lights next to people with high colour . . ." She mentioned that the president's former law partner, Basil O'Connor, president of the

Warm Springs Foundation, had been on hand that day as had been the Canadian ambassador to Washington, Leighton McCarthy, who had a cottage at Warm Springs and of whom the president was fond. Daisy wrote that her cousin "looks ten years older than last year, to me—of course I wouldn't confess that to anyone, least of all to him, but he knows it himself."[45]

Lucy Rutherfurd came over from Aiken, where she had a winter place, and spent time with her friend. By this time Daisy knew very well about the longtime friendship, and despite her liking and admiration for Eleanor Roosevelt was careful not to inform the president's wife, when she saw her, that Lucy occasionally saw the president. At the time of the crisis in relations between Eleanor and Franklin Roosevelt, when in reading her husband's mail while he was suffering from pneumonia after return from England and France in September 1918 Eleanor Roosevelt discovered the affair with Lucy, an arrangement had been made that Franklin would end any romantic relationship, but this arrangement had long since broken down. On a weekend early in July 1944, when the vice presidential issue was heating up, the president was in a hurry to resolve it because he had arranged through Anna, who knew about the meetings and approved, to have dinner with Mrs. Rutherfurd on that Friday night, having seen her the evening before when she arrived in Washington, and the two were to spend the weekend at Shangri-La. September 1, en route from Washington to Hyde Park, the president's train stopped for several hours at Allamuchy, New Jersey, where he met Lucy. She was by then a widow; her husband, long ill, had died the previous month. After she arrived at Warm Springs in late November, Lucy talked with Daisy about their friend's illness. "We understand each other perfectly, I think," the cousin wrote, "and feel the same about F.D.R." Lucy too had begun to worry. The reason was the president's loneliness as well as illness. It was sad to see as attractive an individual as "Franklin" or "F.," as they described him in letters, both lonely and ill. Harry Hopkins had told a friend of Lucy that when he was living in the White House there was evening after evening when Franklin was left entirely alone, but for Hopkins. Lucy thought it better in the last years, for Daisy was there often and Anna had begun living in the White House. "We got to the point of literally weeping on each other's shoulder," Daisy wrote, "& we kissed each other, I think just because we each felt thankful that the other understood & wants to help Franklin!"[46]

Three days later at Warm Springs an untoward situation arose, of which the president was without knowledge. The president's correspondence secretary, Hassett, had been present that day and wrote in his diary for December 6, Wednesday, "Quiet day at the Foundation. After signing his mail, the President went for a swim in the pool—the old one at the foot of the hill—his first swim on this trip. Friends from the Foundation with him for dinner." This was not quite the whole story of that day, nor did Daisy, the other diarist on the scene, understand much more than Hassett. Her diary was more detailed, more descriptive. She began it auspiciously, "A very good day for the Pres." It had been cloudy but without wind, she wrote, and so "F" had decided to go swimming. A longtime patient, Mrs. Pearson, was in the enclosed pool when the president and Daisy arrived, and it was warm in the pool, although only perhaps 83–84° rather than the 89° when the water came out of the ground. Everything seemed all right. Roosevelt got to talking with Mrs. Pearson about the old times and then about his muscles. He tried to walk, and discovered his hips were stiff and thought that unless he loosened them he would not be able to stand for his inauguration. He told Daisy afterward he believed he could do that by lying flat on a board, legs hanging over, and thus stretch the front hip muscles. Dr. Bruenn had wanted the president to stay in the pool only ten minutes, and Daisy was watching the time, but the president was enjoying himself and talking with Mrs. Pearson, and they did not get him out until after twenty minutes. They all combined to keep him warm on his way back to the fireplace, and he had only good reactions, Daisy concluded. "He ate a *real* lunch, with *real* appetite, taking two helpings of everything and after lunch he was completely relaxed, & had a sound sleep until almost 4." Dorothy Brady came in, and FDR worked on the mail until half past six, too long, Daisy felt. A couple named Irwin and Dr. Bruenn came to dinner. As usual the president did all the talking, and looked tired when they finally left, a little "too much and too long," although Daisy concluded that one social day would not harm him if not repeated.[47]

What the president and Daisy did not know was that when Bruenn took the president's pressure, following the swimming, it showed an alarming rise, higher than the pressure at the Quebec Conference. It was 260/150 mm Hg.

For the rest of the time in Warm Springs the illness of the president went along as best it could. For whatever reason, and because of the appalling blood pressure reading of December 6 it is difficult to imagine what produced the comment, Dr. Bruenn seems to have said something encouraging to Daisy. It may have been only some comment about how hungry the president had been after he overexerted in the pool. Daisy wrote Lucy, and the latter wrote back about the "good news." Lucy had been hoping, she said, for word from Roosevelt, and none had come. But then after the good news it soon seemed he was back to the old experiences, feeling "logy" or down. Daisy hated to see company arrive, as when Dr. Bruenn and Dr. Duncan from Bethesda together with George Fox came in one evening at about half past nine. She knew Duncan's nominal errand, to look over the polio hospital, which the navy was using, was not the real reason; he was looking over the president. That evening she had worked hard to get the president quiet and relaxed, and he was dictating something to her when the three men came in. He immediately became the charming host, laughed and told stories, teased Bruenn, keying himself up to create the scene he desired.[48]

Two days later, December 15, Bob Hannegan of the national committee arrived for lunch, scheduled for one o'clock with the president all set to say good-bye in an hour, but it was a quarter after three when Hannegan left. One could hardly blame Hannegan; it was a long way from Washington to Georgia to spend a single hour with the president. Hannegan had just led the party through a victorious election and had much on his mind. Daisy could not do anything about the length of the chairman's stay, other than complain to her diary. "The more I see the Pres. the more convinced I am that the only way he can live," she wrote, "is by having *shorter* sessions, and repeated rests in between—It is probably the heart, for he gets so tired-looking & grey, but looks 100% better after a rest."[49]

4 ▪ *Yalta and Warm Springs*

By the turn of the new year, the last year that Roosevelt would see, perhaps a strangely sounding year if compared to the high Victorian era, the 1880s, when he was born, his life was running out fast, and little remained save attendance at the Yalta Conference in early February and then, upon return, the final trip to Warm Springs. The people around him realized he was in an uncertain position, so far as concerned his health. Budget Director Smith who saw him regularly was not sure what to think of his conference on January 4, 1945. He came away "with the impression more deeply ingrained than ever of the tremendous burden being carried by the President of the United States. He seemed a little more stooped than usual. His face was a bit more tired and the cigarette holder did not seem to have its usual jaunty tilt. . . . he appeared as a man who while in possession of his very great faculties seemed tired in using them."[1]

Jonathan Daniels, newly commissioned, thought him worse, and found his fear confirmed by the scraggly signature of the president on his commission. It was a signature that turned upward strangely, showing that Roosevelt could not hold his wrist steady enough to move a pen in a straight line. It was a signature of a sort that marks many individuals who are terminally ill.

But each day as it began and ended in the first weeks of January 1945 showed that the presidency of Roosevelt, so familiar for so many years, offered no sure evidence that it was coming to an end. Routine, therefore, took over. And routine carried its own assurance: the people around Roosevelt trusted that what they had known would continue.

1

The new year at first gave promise of better times for the president, for several reasons. One was the fact that upon return to the White House he had Anna with him, all the time. She had moved into the mansion. Anna's presence indeed must have made the president feel better. Everyone said that. She had a way of getting things done. Several years later Admiral Leahy told Jonathan Daniels that "Anna could do more for her father in those last days than anybody else. We would suggest he give work to us to do and he would say he would but would not stick to it. Anna could make him." Steve Early told Ickes in 1948 that for the most part the family was unhelpful, but Anna "became her father's housekeeper and did a good job."[2]

Another reason for feeling better was provided by Daisy, who around the turn of the year managed to find a healer, Harry Setaro, whose nickname was Lenny, to help the president.[3] Ardent as she could be, she obtained his name from Mlle Gassette. Lenny was something of a character. He had been a prizefighter in Philadelphia, using the name of Harry Lenny, and later a manager, serving in the corner when Joe Louis won the world championship. He had turned to healing through massage. He had rubbed various people, from the writer Damon Runyon in California to the head of International Business Machines, Thomas J. Watson, in New York. At Daisy's behest Lenny went to work on the president's legs, while FDR was visiting Daisy on December 28 at her house, known as Wilderstein, and after working on the president's feet ended with a smiling assurance, "President, you're going to walk!" A few days later, January 2, she had Fox over to be sure he approved Lenny's course of therapy. The president said he had his fingers crossed as to whether Admiral McIntire would approve. That evening McIntire was working on Roosevelt's nose, and the president said casually to the doctor, "I've got a new thing in massage, have you heard?"

The doctor said, "So I hear."

The president continued, "It's all right, too."

"So I hear," said the doctor.[4]

Lenny's appearance and his treatments—he saw Roosevelt perhaps a dozen times, and treated him until he went to Warm Springs for the last time—must have provided a little comic relief for the urbane president, quite apart from what the treatments accomplished. Years later Lenny told his story, and it gives a sense of what he must have told the president. "Now I'm a little scared," he said at the beginning of his account. "I'm not exactly scared because I'm sure of myself and I know my gift but here I am a lousy prize fighter treatin' the President of the United States." He began by asking the president how he felt, and finally said, "Well, Prez, let's get to work." In Lenny's words, "I try to locate the trouble and I locate it. I say to him, 'Prez, you never had infantile paralysis and you don't have it now.' 'Just as I thought,' replied FDR, 'just as I thought.' " According to Lenny the initial treatment lasted two and a half hours. "All of a sudden he says, 'Daisy . . . I can move my little toe.' He's all excited. I say, 'Prez, what are you tryin' to do? Kid me?' "

After the Yalta Conference, Lenny went to Hyde Park to give him another treatment, and Daisy said, "Harry, the President gives you credit for getting him to Yalta in the condition he was in." Lenny related that he gave the president several treatments at Hyde Park and six more in Washington, the last on March 25—which must have been quite a success, as Lenny described it, for "now I got him movin' his legs. Not just his toes. His legs. 'I feel swell,' he says to me the last time. 'I feel so good that if I could stand up I'd like to box you three rounds.' I says, 'Prez, when you come back from Warm Springs we'll box three rounds sittin' in chairs and meanwhile I'll see Mike Jacobs about puttin' us on a three-round exhibition . . .' "

The masseur possessed a considerable shrewdness, and while at work noticed one characteristic of his patient that many more sophisticated people failed to see. "He had a funny way of saying 'Oh, really?' " he related to a friendly newspaperman a year and more after the president passed on. "For instance, if I told you I could jump across the Delaware River you'd say 'don't give me that baloney, Lenny.' The President would just say, 'Oh, really?' You knew he didn't believe you, and yet he wasn't saying so."[5]

Lenny offered occasional medical opinions, which may have had something to do with McIntire's noncommittal stance. The president ventured to Lenny that he had lost a little weight since returning from Warm Springs in November–December 1944. Lenny said that of course he lost weight, that his spleen was "eating him up," and promised to get the spleen and other allied organs functioning.

During Lenny's work with FDR, Daisy began a course of her own with the president, starting him on lemon and honey in hot water before breakfast every morning.

Years later Dorothy Brady told the editor of Daisy's diary, Geoffrey C. Ward, that among members of the president's staff there was considerable hostility toward Daisy. "We all turned against her when she got that strange fellow onto the scene. We were scared of him, messing with the President's treatment like that." Daisy cared not a whit what the staff felt.[6]

January 16, back in Washington from Hyde Park, the president must have lost his enthusiasm for Lenny. On January 18 he was in his office in the west wing working on a speech with Grace Tully, Dorothy Brady, Rosenman, and Sherwood. He suddenly stopped, looked around, and asked, "What in this room reminds you the most of me?" Grace Tully named a naval print, Mrs. Brady a portrait of John Paul Jones. The president dictated little notes beginning, "In the event of my death . . ." and had them put in the safe. When Mrs. Brady returned from the final trip to Warm Springs she found the Jones portrait waiting for her. Daisy, who was present, received a painting of the Statue of Liberty; she had been a nurse on Ellis Island during World War I.

On the day before the inauguration the president held a cabinet meeting, and he looked bad. Frances Perkins, secretary of labor, had made an arrangement with him to leave the cabinet at the end of the president's term, and came to the cabinet meeting prepared for it to be her last formal session as a cabinet member. In the morning she had sent him a note apprising him that this was her last cabinet meeting—so he could make reference to it during the meeting, as was his custom. He did not make reference. She arranged to see him afterward to remind him. Several other cabinet members so arranged, and she was last, because that was her order of precedence—the Labor Department had been established later than all the other cabinet departments. It was nearly four o'clock when she got in, and she was shocked, for the pallor in his face, the blue lips, reminded her of a hospital room, even though he was sitting in a chair, not lying on a hospital bed. He held his head in his hands and looked at her wearily. She stated her case, and he became almost emotional, put her hand on his and said that she had done so well, accomplished so much, and he did not wish her to depart at that moment, that he needed to find a replacement and could not think of one, that he wanted to put off the problem. He thanked her for her work—something he rarely did (Hopkins once told President Truman's press secretary, Charles Ross, that Roosevelt only once had ever thanked him for anything). With this Miss Perkins rang for the receptionist, William D. Simmons, and whispered to him that the president was tired and needed to lie down. She said the same thing to Grace Tully, who also had noticed that he was not looking well.[7]

The fourth inaugural, next day, January 20, was undoubtedly something of an anticlimax—the election itself, in November, had been more exhilarating—but it must have given the president something of a lift, like Anna's presence in the White House and for a while the presence of Lenny the healer. It marked the end of a difficult and long labor, preparing the country for the fourth term. The third term had created many difficulties in proposing and managing it. The fourth was in some ways worse, for the Republicans had spoken of tiredness. The ceremony itself brought the whole business to an end. It was a relatively simple affair. There was no need, as in the past, to parade up Pennsylvania Avenue to the Capitol and endure a vast crowd of onlookers. Because of the war and the need for economy, White House aides related, the fourth inaugural was held on the south portico, with guests standing in the mud and slush and snow. The president stood in his braces, not at all easy for him. The weather was raw. He insisted on giving his address without an overcoat or even his cape. But his speech was the shortest inaugural address on record, a few dozen words. Dr. Bruenn, watching carefully, wrote in his diary that the president got through the address quite easily.

He did not look well that day. James Roosevelt wrote that before the speech he suffered another attack similar to that aboard the train in San Diego, and that the two of them, father and son, again suffered it out, nothing the worse, and the guests and servants and staff who did not see the president in agony were the better for not knowing. One must doubt—given Anna's disbelief—if the episode happened. But there were people who did testify as to the president's appearance. The soon-to-be attorney general in the Truman administration, later associate justice of the Supreme Court, and at the time a leading official in the Justice Department, Tom Clark, saw Roosevelt give the inaugural speech: "Oh, he looked terrible," Clark remembered. "To me he looked terrible. I couldn't even talk to him, I was distressed." During the White House luncheon for a select group of invitees that followed, the guests had opportunity to observe the president close at hand. "He looks exactly as my husband did when he went into his decline," said Mrs. Woodrow Wilson. "Don't say that to another soul," cautioned Frances Perkins. "He has a great and terrible job to do, and he's got to do it, even if it kills him."[8]

After the inaugural came the Yalta Conference, a long trip to an exotic place in the Soviet Union, on the Black Sea, and for part of the journey a sea voyage. The president could look forward to that. He always liked trips, and especially voyages. The trip across the Atlantic aboard a sister ship of the cruiser *Baltimore*, the USS *Quincy*, took the presidential party to Gibraltar and thence to Malta. Aboard ship the first few days the weather was rough, which never bothered the president, an excellent sailor. He occupied the captain's quarters, his daughter, Anna, the admiral's quarters where movies were shown every night, with the president always in attendance. At the outset the fare was *Our Hearts Were Young and Gay, Here Come the Waves*, and *The Lady in the Window*, the last being the best up to that time, Anna opined, the others being "lousy."[9] Thereafter *The Princess and the Pirate*, and on January 27 *Fighting Lady*. On the twenty-eighth and twenty-ninth it was *Laura* and *To Have and Have Not*. On the thirtieth, the president's birthday, there was no movie but a celebration, for which rival groups of bakers aboard, including FDR's Filipino mess men, baked five cakes. Three were the same size, representing the first three terms, and a huge cake represented the fourth term, and finally a little cake with a large question mark made of frosting in the center represented a possible fifth term. Another day Roosevelt watched a field meet on the ship's fantail, with battles royal, tugs-of-war, and three-legged races. Lieutenant Rigdon, aboard, wrote of how the president talked, laughed, told stories, and was lively at predinner cocktail parties. He rested and read, although not noticeably more than usual.[10] He did, incidentally, read the State Department's bulky briefing papers. His "assistant president," Byrnes, angry because of the president's failure to support him for the vice presidency, later claimed he did not. The president's daughter, Anna, years later wrote an inquiring historian to the contrary.[11]

At Malta the president held a short conference with Prime Minister Churchill, toured the island, and then the two leaders together with the several hundred Americans and Britons accompanying them enplaned for the Soviet Union. Well into the night the big planes rose into the air and turned toward the east, with the president's plane one of the last, accompanied by five fighters during a flight that took the nation's chief executive and a few of his principal staff members across the Greek islands and Turkey. Dr. Bruenn remembered how he, the doctor, slept sitting down, his back against the president's bed at the rear of the "Sacred Cow"; he slept that way so in event of a sudden change of course, perhaps to avoid antiaircraft fire from German batteries, the president would not roll helplessly and fall, deadweight, to the floor. Fortunately all was well, and the planes arrived safely at the airport at Saki, the president sleeping fitfully during much of the seven-hour, fourteen-hundred-mile flight.[12]

There followed a rough five-hour automobile ride over eighty miles of barely passable roads from the airfield to Yalta, where the president was installed in a villa built by the last Romanov, Nicholas II, in 1911. The U.S. Navy's medics had fumigated the place to rid it of lice, and worked over the bathroom facilities. Furnishings, including silverware and table service, came from wherever the Soviet hosts could find them, some from Moscow itself.

Admiral Leahy was at Yalta and in his book of diary entries and reminiscences, *I Was There*, remarked his surprise that at the beginning of the conference sessions Roosevelt asked him to attend the political meetings, for he long had felt that the president possessed virtually a photographic memory. Leahy had not seen any deterioration of FDR's health. After Roosevelt's death he thought that at Yalta the president might have had a premonition that he might not be present at the end of the war and needed a witness; the president's alter ego, Hopkins, was present, but had been ill for months in 1944, was drinking at Yalta, and his prospect of survival, Leahy thought, was unpromising.[13]

But it is difficult to put much credence in Leahy's guess that FDR invited him to the political meetings because of what the future might hold. Leahy made only penciled notes on a few questions arising at meetings of the Big Three, often in haste. Byrnes was present at Yalta and because he once had been a court stenographer made shorthand notes when present at sessions. Roosevelt may have invited Leahy just to fill out the table.

When the president arrived in the Crimea his health was adjudged both good and bad, depending upon the observer. Secretary of State Stettinius wrote in his diary for February 2, "The president seemed rested and calm and said he had gotten plenty of sleep on the way here. He said he had been resting ten hours every night since leaving Washington but still couldn't understand why he was not slept out." Churchill's personal physician, the lugubrious Moran, was far less confident. He reported that people who attended a dinner given by the president agreed that Roosevelt had "gone to bits." Moran included a criticism of the president's abilities in general. "If he has sometimes been short of facts about the subject under discussion his shrewdness has covered this up. Now, they say, the shrewdness has gone, and there is nothing left." He doubted whether the president was "fit for his job here." Three days later he again set out a medical and political diagnosis:

> To a doctor's eye, the President appears a very sick man. He has all the symptoms of hardening of the arteries of the brain in an advanced stage, so that I give him only a few months to live. But men shut their eyes when they do not want to see, and the Americans here cannot bring themselves to believe that he is finished. His daughter thinks he is not really ill, and his doctor [probably McIntire; both he and Bruenn were present] backs her up.[14]

How to equate these judgments? Admiral Leahy felt that Roosevelt conducted the Crimean conference with "great skill" and that as presiding officer he "dominated" discussions. If he looked fatigued at the conference's end, so did everyone else. Yalta, the admiral wrote, was one of the most strenuous weeks he had ever experienced. In preparation for Admiral McIntire's book Bruenn was asked by his former superior to write his memories of Roosevelt, and the resultant letter stressed the president's mental acuity at Yalta, that his mind constantly was at work. The medical historian Dr. Park has concluded that Roosevelt lost nothing at Yalta, that the commentaries of later years based on his nearness to death were wrong. Park scores

Roosevelt's critics for saying the president gave away U.S. positions, and contends that his behavior was evidence of a focused FDR.[15]

Charles E. Bohlen, State Department liaison with the White House and the president's interpreter at Yalta, similarly saw no loss during the work of the conference: "Although Roosevelt was not a well man at Yalta and certainly did not have his normal degree of energy and health, I do not know of any case where he really gave away anything to the Soviets because of this ill health. He seemed to be guided very heavily by his advisers and took no step independently."[16]

To the present writer Roosevelt's behavior at Yalta seems un-exceptionable. The conference dealt with essentially four issues: (1) voting arrangements in the new United Nations; (2) general policy toward the liberated governments of Eastern Europe, and specific policy toward the postwar government of Poland; (3) the immediate postwar governance of Germany; and (4) Russia's joining the war against Japan. Of these issues, arrangements pertaining to the UN were of minor importance—the Soviets asked for and received three seats in the General Assembly, but the latter organization was not foreseen as a place for decision, only as a forum, and its later huge membership, what with admission of new nations in the Caribbean, Africa, and Asia, made the Soviets' three seats of little meaning. Eastern Europe and Poland lay within the Russian sphere because of presence of the Red Army, and there was little the West could do about what the Soviets desired within their own bailiwick. In the allotment of zones in Germany the Anglo-American armies occupied the industrial heartland, a far larger prize than the agricultural Soviet zone. As for soliciting Soviet assistance in the conquest of Japan, at the time it seemed the thing to do; there was little disagreement over the issue within the American delegation, and only later did it begin to appear of less importance.

The president admittedly possessed a basic weakness in foreign policy, and this was, as Bohlen acutely remarked, his willingness to rely on "instinctive grasp" of a subject, his willingness to play hunches. In domestic affairs the willingness did him little harm and probably brought a good deal of success, because his domestic hunches were good. In foreign affairs they were not so good. He traveled during the presidency, far more than any previous president, and had traveled earlier in his life, but he possessed a traveler's knowledge, nothing profound. Nor did he obtain much from reading books. He was not a reader. Postmaster General Walker believed he had never read a book (Walker heard that someone asked the president if he had read *Forever Amber*, the naughty novel of 1944, and the presidential response was, "Only the dirty parts"). He preferred learning from people. In foreign affairs, particularly when dealing with Soviet leaders, Bohlen wrote, instinct was the president's way, and "this style meant a lack of precision, which . . . was a serious fault." A deeper knowledge of history, and the reactions of foreign peoples, would have helped. "Helpful, too, would have been more study of the position papers prepared by American experts, more attention to detail . . ."[17]

Fortunately the president's hunches in foreign affairs, his superficialities, were not in evidence during the Yalta Conference, by all means the most important, if still lacking in decisiveness, of the three wartime Big Three meetings—Teheran (November–December 1943), Yalta, and Potsdam (July–August 1945). To be sure, at Yalta the president quite probably was too tired to make any excursions in policy.

At Yalta the president's health, despite his safety in matters of policy, was parlous. After a set-to during a Big Three session on February 8 on the subject of Poland—Poland's postwar borders and government took more time at Yalta than any other subject—the president that night suffered *pulsus alternans*, in which strong and weak beats alternated, caused by a combination of heart and blood pressure. Bruenn was really worried. "That's a very bad sign," he recalled. "We certainly put the clamps on him by cutting down his activities for the next 24 hours . . ." The physician stopped the all-day activity. Everything turned out all right; the alternating pulse "disappeared, thank goodness, after three or four days," a transient episode. To the interviewer Brenda Heaster he added, "It indicated that he didn't have much reserve."[18]

At Yalta, in addition to Bruenn and McIntire, the president was subject to careful watching by Anna. To her husband at that time, John Boettiger, in uniform back in Washington as an aide to the president, she wrote a remarkable letter that has survived, worth quoting for what it shows of how Roosevelt's illness was being managed:

Just between you and me, we are having to watch OM [the old man, her father] very carefully from the physical standpoint. He gets all wound up, seems to thoroughly enjoy it all, but wants too many people around, and then won't go to bed early enough. The result is that he doesn't sleep well. Ross and Bruenn are both worried because of the old "ticker" trouble—which, of course, no one knows about but those two and me. I am working closely with Ross and Bruenn, and am using all the ingenuity and tact I can muster to try to separate the wheat from the chaff—to keep the unnecessary people out of OM's room and to steer the necessary ones in at the best times. This involves trying my best to keep abreast as much as possible of what is actually taking place at the Conf[erence] so that I will know who should and who should not see OM. I have found out thru Bruenn (who won't let me tell Ross that I know) that this "ticker" situation is far more serious than I ever knew. And the biggest difficulty in handling the situation here is that we can, of course, tell no one of the "ticker" trouble. It's truly worrisome—and there's not a heluva lot anyone can do about it. (Better tear off and destroy this paragraph.)[19]

After the conference, photographs of the principals as well as the other attendees were sent back for distribution to news agencies, and Daniels picked out the best. "Some of them," he remembered, "were appalling. I must admit that as part of the protective mechanism, I picked only those pictures which seemed to me to be the best ones of Franklin Roosevelt."[20] Some of the photographs were taken outdoors, where weather intervened and it was difficult to control results, and all of them were hasty. The photographers were members of the Army Signal Corps and not as skilled as Tames, who had taken the photograph of a handsome Roosevelt sitting under Jackson's magnolia tree. Too, several months had passed since that day.

On the return trip aboard the *Quincy*, the president enjoyed meeting Ibn Saud of Saudi Arabia in the Great Bitter Lake, and meeting the two other monarchs, King Farouk of Egypt and Emperor Haile Selassie of Ethiopia, who came to the same rendezvous to make his acquaintance.

Bohlen saw the president at Algiers in order to show him incoming cables, and believed his weariness was apparent to all. FDR's hand shook so much he could hardly hold a piece of paper. Yet it did not occur to Bohlen that the president was near death, nor as he recalled did anyone mention the president's health. Bohlen would have liked to have asked Hopkins, whom he knew, about the tiredness and shaking hands, but Hopkins had left the ship to fly home to enter the Mayo Clinic. The State Department's representative did not have sufficiently close relations with Admiral Leahy to bring up such a sensitive subject.[21]

Roosevelt did little work on the way home. Admiral McIntire wrote that he hoped Roosevelt would have a chance to rest aboard ship, but that hope, he said, went glimmering when Judge Rosenman boarded the *Quincy* at Algiers. FDR had summoned him to help write the presidential report to Congress, and the admiral wrote that every morning and part of each afternoon the two worked on the Yalta speech. It was a piece of drudgery, and after Rosenman brought the dictated matter into shape the president went over it, line by line. But in an oral history Rosenman told his interviewer that when he boarded the president's ship he had a first draft of the Yalta speech and could not get FDR to work on it. "He would sit up on the top deck with his daughter Anna most of the day, and in the evening he would go to the stateroom. He loved caviar, and old Stalin had stuffed caviar there as though it were ballast, and he enjoyed the caviar. . . . He only worked on the speech the last day or two and then finished it in the White House."[22]

The pool reporter for the International News Service, Bob Nixon, picked up the ship at Algiers and remembered that Roosevelt was failing—"how thin, haggard, and gray he looked"—although the reporter had lunch with him one day and he seemed in good spirits, good voice, and lucid. Nixon, like Rosenman, saw him sitting on the admiral's deck one flight above the main deck with his dark blue cloak around him and his battered, gray felt hat. "He would sit there for hours, motionless, just staring, with his own thoughts perhaps. We knew he was a sick man."[23] He may have been thinking about his military aide, the genial Pa Watson, who had suffered a cerebral hemorrhage and died. Watson had been with the president for a long time.

A testimony to how fragile the president's condition was appeared in another of Anna Roosevelt's letters to her husband, written in anticipation of Rosenman's arrival aboard ship. Fortunately for Anna, and the president even more so, Rosenman's presence did not require any presidential time. "OM is standing up under it all extremely well—since that one scare I wrote you about," Anna informed her correspondent. "My worry now is that apparently Sam is meeting us so as to work on the way home on a possible message to Congress and a definite radio speech—and OM should really spend the entire crossing resting up. My fear is, of course, that he will have a terrific let-down when he gets home, and possibly crack under it as he did last year. But, all we can do is hold our fingers crossed."[24]

The voyage at last was over, and the presidential train arrived in Union Station, early in the morning of February 28, and the limousine took the chief executive out to the White House. Hassett and Daniels were on hand, together with other staffers, and the two went up the elevator to the private rooms on the second floor and heard about Watson's illness and death while the president with Mrs. Roosevelt were waiting for breakfast to be sent up. Hassett had been gloomy about the president, but this time told his diary he "has come home in the pink of condition—hasn't looked better in a year. The long journey homeward has given him a chance for much-needed rest and relaxation. His color good and spirits high." Daniels afterward said the same to reporters.[25]

March 1 the president delivered his report to Congress. He opened with a most unaccustomed reference to his crippled condition: "Mr. Vice President, Mr. Speaker, Members of the Congress, I hope that you will pardon me for the unusual posture of sitting down during the presentation of what I want to say, but I know that you will realize it makes it a lot easier for me in not having to carry about ten pounds of steel around the bottom of my legs . . ." The speech may not have been as bad as the Bremerton address, but it was close. Rosenman went up to the Capitol to hear it and was dismayed, partly because of the halting, ineffective manner of delivery, also because the president ad-libbed—the judge had never heard him do it more. "Some of his extemporaneous remarks were wholly irrelevant, and some of them almost bordered on the ridiculous . . ."[26]

2

Well before the trip down to Warm Springs the president's failing health was evident to everyone who saw him. If Hassett thought

Roosevelt looked good upon the return from Yalta, he soon changed his mind. The weeks that followed brought back the old gray color in his face and widened the dark circles around his eyes. Rest seemed the sole presidential desire. FDR called up Daisy in Rhinebeck on March 14 or thereabouts and said he was tired and wanted to get off to Warm Springs on the twenty-sixth or twenty-seventh. He would leave from Hyde Park and desired only to "sleep & sleep & sleep." During the trip he did not plan for "anything at any time." March 15 he called in the evening and said he was alone in his study, would go to bed in a little while, and had first to clean up a pile of paper—correspondence and memos and reports—on a chair. He said he was "suffering from exhaustion."[27]

The president celebrated his fortieth wedding anniversary—he had been married on Saint Patrick's Day, 1905. For the evening he invited the War Food administrator, Judge Marvin Jones of Texas, an old friend with whom he felt familiar, Ambassador McCarthy of Canada, and Justice Robert H. Jackson of the Supreme Court and Mrs. Jackson. Jones noticed that the president did not say much while Mrs. Roosevelt carried on the conversation. "Then he would want to dip in and he would brighten up and seem himself for a moment, and then I would notice his head would drop down." Mrs. Jackson told Jones years later that after leaving the dinner she had said to her husband, "We're not going to have Mr. Roosevelt with us very long." Justice Jackson stopped the car and said, "Why do you say that?" She asked her husband if he had seen how the president looked, how he dropped his head down after he said a few words.[28]

The president's last press conference, March 20, his 997th conference, seemed to an onlooker who sat just behind him, the public relations counsel David Noyes, who was helping out at the White House, a masterful performance, with Roosevelt bright and alert, in control, performing brilliantly. But there was a telltale preliminary that Noyes never forgot, attesting to increasing physical debility. The president was trying to light a cigarette, and put the cigarette in his holder to light it in the usual way. Unable to connect the match, his hand shaking badly, he opened the desk drawer, placed his bent elbow inside, partly closed the drawer, and got a firm hold on his hand.[29]

It was about this time that Daniels, going up in mornings to see the president in bed, pajamas covered with a bed robe and sitting bolt upright, not easy for a man whose hips and legs were of no use, regularly saw the electrocardiograph machine near the president's quarters off the blue oval room on the second floor.[30]

There was something else Roosevelt was suffering from during this period after the return from Yalta, and that was lapses of memory. Mackenzie King came to the White House for a short stay and found the president repeated himself. At a luncheon he told King about Byrnes, who had married "a Presbyterian girl" (she was an Episcopalian). Having left the Catholic Church, Byrnes was singing in the choir, the president said. If Byrnes had been the president's running mate in the 1944 election, he told King, it would have cost him one or two million Catholic votes. He had told this story the night before at dinner. He told about Churchill's being in Miami and going for a swim, the waves rolling him over, determined he would get the better of them, and finally having to get out of the water defeated. Next night he repeated the story. King thought the president's wife and daughter were embarrassed by these repetitions, but no one said anything.[31]

During these weeks Asst. Secy. of State Nelson A. Rockefeller, future governor of New York, put before the president a memorandum, so Bohlen learned, proposing an invitation to Argentina to become a founding member of the UN. It was a direct breach of an agreement at Yalta, according to which only nations that declared war on Germany could be founding members. Argentina did not qualify. Roosevelt signed the memo without understanding its content.[32]

Anna one day had a long, disturbing talk with Daniels. She reported how Byrnes had behaved badly at Yalta (he had taken umbrage that he was not invited to an important political meeting that the president had chosen to denominate a military session). She was concerned about the strain such goings-on placed on her father and said Dr. Bruenn had told her that her father must greatly restrict his activities. She broached her plan, that the president was to see only a few people. Daniels, she said, would see those individuals who wanted to see the president and pass their business to Anna and her husband. They would make these secondary decisions without burdening the president, who would handle only the greatest problems.

Daniels was appalled, and apparently was able to pass the proposition off in some way or other, perhaps by stalling. He may only have had to listen to it, for Anna seems to have been thinking of it rather than proposing to start it.[33] Having been a youth during the Wilson administration, and because his father was a cabinet member aware of what happened after Wilson's stroke, when Mrs. Wilson and Dr. Grayson formed a sort of regency, with the president's wife taking the requests of cabinet members to her husband's sickbed and emerging with short comments in her own hand of what the president desired, Daniels knew this sort of arrangement would not work. Mrs. Wilson had become known as the country's only woman president; critics described her as the presidentress. Grayson received much criticism, especially after the president's dismissal of Secy. of State Robert Lansing early in 1920—for Lansing had suggested that Wilson be declared incompetent.

All the while the president's wife was not acting in a helpful way. Dr. Bruenn had gotten together the family members—Mrs. Roosevelt, Anna, and Anna's husband—and told them in no uncertain terms that they must be careful not to place any strain on the president. Daisy always wrote respectfully of Mrs. Roosevelt but noticed about this time that although she was very sweet and charming, she was making the president's life difficult. When FDR on March 25 was visiting at Wilderstein he looked bad, so tired that every word seemed an effort. The presidential couple stayed about a quarter of an hour, with Mrs. Roosevelt doing her best to get him out of the house, back to Hyde Park to see some people at six o'clock, and more people for dinner. "He just can't stand this strain indefinitely," she wrote. She thanked heaven he was scheduled to leave Hyde Park the following Wednesday night, spend a long day in Washington, and thence entrain for Georgia. What she did not learn was that after the president got down to his supposed refuge, only two weeks after Bruenn delivered his lecture, a telephone call came in about half past eight or nine o'clock one evening. By chance Bruenn was in the bedroom talking to the president. The call was from Mrs. Roosevelt. Bruenn told the historian Brenda Heaster years later:

> They were always very polite to each other. She had been to a meeting called "Young Yugoslavia," and she had been really greatly moved by the deplorable condition of the partisan group and so forth who were fighting the Germans. She insisted that the president send supplies and arms to help them. He explained

to her very calmly and clearly that there was no way of getting the stuff in there. Impossible. She insisted. And for the next several minutes she was after him to do this. He was always polite and said "I'm sorry Eleanor but I can't do it."

The doctor took the president's blood pressure after this conversation, and it was markedly elevated, fifty points higher than earlier readings. The veins stood out on his forehead. She had talked for forty-five minutes.[34]

Not long after the president died, Anna told Postmaster General Walker of an incident in November 1944 when Roosevelt also had been in Warm Springs. FDR had just appointed Stettinius secretary of state, and William L. Clayton, a Texas cotton merchant, and Nelson Rockefeller as assistant secretaries. According to Anna her mother called her father and told him what she believed would be the repercussions of these appointments and "raised the devil with him," particularly about appointing Clayton. Anna said, "Father hung up the phone on mother."[35]

Concerning Mrs. Roosevelt, who whatever her many virtues was not a restful person, Dr. Bruenn told the present writer that for a while he had seen Mrs. Roosevelt professionally and discovered she suffered from a low metabolism. Dorothy Bruenn interrupted to ask if he was sure such was the case. He avowed it was, and said he had run the test again. "Just imagine," he added, with a smile, "what she would have been like if she had been up to par!"

At long last the president left Hyde Park, arriving in Washington next morning, March 29, and spent the day with accumulated paperwork. Daniels and Archibald MacLeish of the State Department took a paper in for approval, and FDR wearily made a correction in the first paragraph. After they went out they saw that the correction wrecked the rest of the paper, and had to go back and have him remove the error.

That night the president's staff boarded the train with considerable hope, and the president himself seemed to revive as the national capital receded, perhaps with a sense that the duties that had plagued him were receding as the wheels of the Ferdinand Magellan crossed the joints in the rails with the usual banging noise, as if a hammer were striking something.

The only untoward sign on the way down was when the president came off the train at Warm Springs and was slipped into the front seat of his automobile. Ordinarily when he passed from wheelchair to automobile seat he managed to help the Secret Service men by balancing himself after they lifted him up, turning so he could almost collapse into the seat. This time he was deadweight, and it was all Mike Reilly could do to get him into the automobile. As Mike maneuvered, the president's head rolled strangely, and people who were watching gasped.

The drive from the station to the Little White House, the simple, small cottage that the president had had built for his visits, required only a few minutes. Upon entering the house he appeared to be so tired that he did nothing save sit in a chair with a book in his hands. Finally he went into his bedroom for a rest.[36]

Nothing more of moment occurred until the time came for the end, but behind appearances there was plenty of concern. The night after arrival, March 30, Hassett had a talk with Bruenn. "He is slipping away from us," he said, "and no earthly power can keep him here." Bruenn demurred, asking why he thought so. Hassett answered that he had warned of the same thing when they were last at Warm Springs, in November–December. Hassett said he had worried about FDR's indifference after the Chicago convention, for the president did not act like a man who "cared a damn" about the election. Then Roosevelt had gotten angry at Dewey, had gotten his "Dutch" up. Yet during the campaign in such places as New York City, although he seemed to make it through without trouble, Hassett noticed weariness as Roosevelt handled papers to read or sign. He mentioned the feeble signature—"the old boldness of stroke and liberal use of ink gone, signature often ending in a fadeout." The doctor said that was not important. He admitted that the president was in a precarious condition.[37]

Hassett spoke with Bruenn the next day, March 31, after he had gone to the cottage late that afternoon to obtain a signature on a letter for Byrnes's retirement as director of the Office of War Mobilization and Reconversion. Hassett doubtless had written it; he was an expert with fulsome letters. He told the president Byrnes's retirement was a loss. "Yes," was the answer. "It's too bad some people are so prima-donnaish." He looked bad, said he had lost twenty-five pounds and had no strength or appetite. Bruenn admitted cause for alarm.[38]

Daisy had traveled to Warm Springs with the president, and she quizzed Dr. Bruenn, who confessed to frustration in trying to help the president. Bruenn or Daisy (it is difficult to discern who said this) arranged a program for the president to work without getting tired, and the program lasted three or four days.[39]

Grace Tully, on hand, remembered that FDR had brought down the usual paraphernalia (his stamp collection, including a catalog and equipment) and a long wooden box filled with books he planned to sort out and autograph for deposit in the Hyde Park Library or the "big house" of the estate, as well as the White House. As he worked on the books from the wooden box he used a phrase that later took on a macabre aspect. He would ask his valet, Arthur Prettyman, to move "the coffin" closer to his chair so he could reach it. Several times he spoke of the box as a coffin.[40]

April 6 he ate his evening gruel—Daisy believed gruel was good for him, easy to absorb—and in the midst of it, perhaps tiring of it, wanting it to be absorbed, stopped for a cigarette. He spoke of the San Francisco conference that would draw up the charter for the United Nations, and referred to his part in organization of world peace. He could resign sometime the next year he said, when the UN was a going concern.[41] It is difficult to draw much from this suggestion, for the president liked to talk that way to Daisy. To others, too, he had spoken of his reluctance to continue. It of course was a ritual among American public figures to speak of reluctance: "The office must come to the man." The president may have meant what he said, although in view of the casual way in which he considered the nomination of Truman one must wonder if he had thought of handing over the presidency to a man from Missouri. He would have smiled, even roared with laughter, had he anticipated the expression heard after his death in which political writers announced that power had shifted from the Hudson to the Missouri. Probably he was no more serious about resigning than about describing the long book box as a coffin.

As the days of April 1945 passed, there were signs of improvement. Daisy thought he looked better. The quiet life was doing him good. After lunch there usually was delightful conversation on the president's part, then a nap, followed by a drive in the big car. The drives, she remembered, were through lovely rolling country, the peach trees covered with fruit already as big as walnuts, the sun warm under blue skies—so different from the cold and bleak days of the preceding December. The routine satisfied the president who so much needed quiet.[42]

A happy occasion was the arrival of Lucy. Mrs. Rutherfurd drove in from Aiken and brought along a portrait painter of Russian background, Elizabeth Shoumatoff, and a photographer, a Russian gentleman who had Americanized his name to Robbins. Mrs. Shoumatoff had painted Lucy's friend in 1943, and Lucy wanted another. The president was agreeable. Lucy told Mrs. Shoumatoff her friend was thin and frail but there was something about his face that showed how he had looked when he was young. His features, always handsome, were now chiseled. "I think," she continued, in a low tone, "if this portrait is painted, it should not be postponed."[43]

Years after the president passed on, Mrs. Shoumatoff wrote a charming little memoir about herself in which she said interesting things about Lucy Rutherfurd. The painter had enjoyed a pleasant life in prewar Russia, and left for America during the brief months in 1917 when a republican regime under Alexander Kerensky ruled—or sought to rule—from St. Petersburg. Her husband was in charge of Russian purchases in the United States. Upon arrival everything changed, and the Shoumatoffs became refugees. Her husband drowned while swimming off Long Island at Jones Beach, and the widow took up portrait painting, at which she was immensely successful. Her clients were the very rich, and she did hundreds of portraits, in the course of which she painted Lucy Rutherfurd, which led to the commissions to paint the president. She welcomed the second commission because she was so fond of Lucy. The two had become friends, even though Lucy was a Catholic and Mrs. Shoumatoff was Russian Orthodox. She never sensed any religious difference, for Lucy possessed a wonderful quality of devotion— not merely in religion but in all things, and it could evoke a similar quality in a man. "Lucy was very feminine; she had no extraordinary intellect, but she possessed the most idealistic, almost naive, mind, with a really unselfish, understanding heart."[44]

On April 9, Mrs. Shoumatoff, Robbins, and Lucy set out from Aiken and miscalculated the distance. Meanwhile, the president ordered his car and the Secret Service escort and undertook to meet them. Daisy was with the president, and after eighty-five miles and realizing it was getting late in the afternoon they turned around, toward the setting sun. The president put on his cape and Daisy her raincoat, a good windbreaker. They stopped in front of the drugstore in Manchester for a Coke, and Lucy and her party drove up. Lucy and "Shoumie" got into the president's car, with Daisy in the jump seat, and they all drove home to the Little White House at Warm Springs.

On April 10 sittings began, and Robbins took photographs, which were terrible. He took more the next day, and took the president with cape and without, the latter for the artist, for the painting was to be in the cape. Robbins asked Lucy to pose with the same background, and she sweetly obliged. That afternoon the president and Lucy, Daisy and her cousin Laura Delano, a Secret Service man and the chauffeur, drove around the grounds of the foundation, and Daisy arranged a snap of the group in the automobile, the last picture taken of the president.

Much has been written of April 12, and little more needs to be said. When the artist came in that morning she found the president seated in the designated place with a card table before him covered with papers from the pouch from Washington, which he was going to look through. Mixing her paints she looked carefully at his face and was struck by the good color—the gray appearance was gone. She later learned from doctors that this was a result of the approaching cerebral hemorrhage. She went back to her cottage near that of the president where she and Lucy were staying, and returned with easel, paint box, and board, to find Hassett in the living room with the president, having obtained signatures and spread the papers all over the room, on every chair and table, waiting for his "laundry" to dry. Hassett would write that Mrs. Shoumatoff irritated him during the sittings, distracting the president from his work, measuring the president's nose. In her book the artist said she never measured noses.

Shortly before lunch the butler came in and began setting the table, and the president told him, "We have fifteen minutes more to work."[45] Suddenly he lifted his right hand, passed it over his forehead several times in a strangely jerky way, saying nothing, head bending forward. Only the artist, Lucy, and Daisy were in the room. "Lucy,

Lucy," the artist gasped, "something has happened!" Lucy and Daisy rose to their feet. The president collapsed.

Dr. Bruenn was at the pool, was summoned, and arrived in a few minutes. The president had been carried into his bedroom, from whence people in the living room could hear deep, heavy breathing. Bruenn saw the trouble at once, from dilation of the pupils, the usual things, including the rigid neck, result of a subarachnoid hemorrhage. A good deal of the brain had been damaged. It was "a bolt out of the blue," the doctor remembered, but he was not surprised.[46]

Bruenn called McIntire in Washington, and the latter called Paullin in Atlanta who raced eighty-five miles to Warm Springs in an hour and a half, arriving when the president was in extremis. Bruenn was in the outer room talking to McIntire when he left the telephone, summoned to the bedroom. He began artificial respiration. Heart sounds disappeared. Paullin administered a hypodermic of adrenaline directly to the heart. There were two or three beats and silence. The time was 3:35. Bruenn pronounced the president dead.

January 20, 1945. The president and his wife with thirteen grandchildren.
Franklin D. Roosevelt Library.

January 20, 1945. Fourth inauguration of President Roosevelt, on the south portico of the White House. *National Archives.*

Fourth inaugural. *National Archives.*

Fourth inaugural. Colonel James Roosevelt at right. *National Archives.*

Aboard the heavy cruiser USS *Quincy*, en route to Malta (thence by air to Yalta), the president confers with Admirals King and Leahy, Generals Marshall and Lawrence S. Kuter. *National Archives.*

Malta. The president, James F. Byrnes, Admiral McIntire.
Franklin D. Roosevelt Library.

Aboard the *Quincy*. The president and daughter Anna.
Franklin D. Roosevelt Library.

Malta. The president and Anna, Prime Minister Churchill and daughter Sarah
Oliver. *Franklin D. Roosevelt Library.*

Malta. Admirals Leahy and King, the president, General Marshall.
National Archives.

Yalta. Harry L. Hopkins, Stephen T. Early, Charles E. Bohlen. *National Archives.*

Yalta. Edward J. Flynn.
National Archives.

Yalta. Marshal Stalin and the president. *Franklin D. Roosevelt Library.*

The Big Three at Yalta. *National Archives.*

After Yalta. With King Ibn Saud of Saudi Arabia, aboard the *Quincy* in the Great Bitter Lake. *National Archives.*

King Farouk of Egypt boards the *Quincy*. *National Archives.*

Farouk with the president. *National Archives.*

John G. Winant, ambassador to Great Britain; the president; Secretary of State Edward R. Stettinius, Jr.; and Harry Hopkins, aboard the *Quincy*. *National Archives.*

March 1, 1945. Address to Congress. *Franklin D. Roosevelt Library.*

Warm Springs, March 30–April 12, 1945. Working on the terrace of the Little White House, with Dorothy Brady. Photographed by Margaret Suckley. *Franklin D. Roosevelt Library.*

At the work table before the fireplace, Little White House. Photographed by Margaret Suckley. *Franklin D. Roosevelt Library.*

The president's last photograph, Warm Springs, April 11, 1945. Going for a drive. In front of the Little White House. In back with the president, Margaret Suckley and Laura Delano, in front Charles Fredericks (Secret Service man) and Montgomery Snyder (chauffeur). *Franklin D. Roosevelt Library.*

The Little White House. *National Archives.*

5 ∎ *Conclusion*

*T*here can be no doubt that President Roosevelt's last year in the White House was, physically speaking, something he should not have undertaken. With his cardiovascular disease he was in an impossible position, in which his strength was running out. Despite his intention to hold on, to continue, and perhaps it was the belief of a Hyde Park squire that unlike other individuals he could "make it" by willpower alone, there was in his case no resort, no procedure, that could keep him going. He had been born in the century in which William Henley penned the lines about being the master of one's fate, the captain of one's soul, but even for the Victorians it was an impossibility.

It is true that the president's physicians did not tell him what he was up against, even though he knew its outlines. He could have believed that his cardiovascular disease was not of the worst, that as Bruenn later put the case to a historian the president's condition was critical but not desperate. In what might have amounted almost to a reservoir of hope of the sort that so many ill individuals some-how manage to hold, the president mistakenly but with the best of intentions could have made his decision to take a fourth term. In the lack of communication that assuredly existed between McIntire and Roosevelt could have been the cause of the tragedy in which a president of the United States held on to office far beyond the point when he should have resigned, given up, admitted that infirmity had become too great, beyond his will to change.

But something more was evident in the president's behavior, and it must perforce be considered, even though to attribute such willfulness to the president is an awkward appraisal. This was that as soon as he discovered his real problem he took steps to withhold knowledge of it from as many individuals as possible. He not merely disguised it, he suppressed it.

When Roosevelt's health declined, when illness enveloped him, plaguing his days, vacations bringing no release, the president at first was probably uncertain what to do. Early in 1944 he spoke with Daisy and on one occasion with Boss Flynn of the Bronx about not running for a fourth term. He could have been serious—not trying out an idea on his cousin or his longtime friend but wondering if he could go on. Critics of the president should consider this hesitation; they cannot be certain it was only a show of reluctance. There is some reason to believe he meant it and was trying to appraise his future and that of the country along with it.

Then on March 28, 1944, the confused diagnoses of Admiral McIntire came to an end, and not very long thereafter the president learned what had been ailing him. Until that time it was possible for him to believe McIntire's diagnoses of bronchitis and influenza and postflu and walking pneumonia. From the moment that Bruenn, whose department at Bethesda the president visited, began appearing daily at the White House to minister to the ill president, Roosevelt would have known he was dealing with a "heart man," a specialist. Shortly afterward McIntire asked Bruenn to take over the work of seeing the president, and would have had to make some sort of explanation to the president of the reason for an assistant. This would have given the president opportunity to confirm his own guess that he was a cardiovascular patient. If McIntire spoke about how the work of surgeon general had become so pressing, his duties no longer permitting visits to the White House in mornings and late afternoons or going upon presidential trips, Roosevelt would have seen his chance for an explanation and taken it, inquiring, "Ross, did I not see that young man, Bruenn, at the Electrocardiograph Department at Bethesda?" It is virtually certain that the president learned from McIntire that his heart and arteries were the problem, that Bruenn was "one of the best heart men." From who else would he have known Bruenn's background? On April 11, 1945, when he was at Warm Springs, he received a visit from his Hyde Park neighbor, Secretary Morgenthau, who had dinner with the president and his friends and afterward spent some time chatting with Roosevelt. Morgenthau was keeping a diary, and put down what he said to the president and vice versa. He told the president, among other things, that his wife, Elinor, a close friend of the president's wife, was suffering from heart trouble and had been a patient at Columbia Presbyterian. Roosevelt said that he, FDR, knew a heart specialist at Columbia Presbyterian.

Having discovered his physical problem, it is clear that the president determined to dominate this new situation. In the case of McIntire he had no difficulty holding control. The admiral's statements about Roosevelt's health—that the president was as medically fit as one could expect for a man of his age, in excellent health, nothing wrong except bronchitis and a few minor and allied problems, prognosis excellent—in retrospect seem inspired. All that was necessary to ensure McIntire's cooperation would have been a few remarks such as that for any illness of the nation's commander in chief to be made known would have compromised national security, that it was necessary for the president's position that there be no talk about replacing him. McIntire was beholden to Roosevelt for rapid advance, from lieutenant commander to vice admiral. If he had opposed the president he would have had to resign, unthinkable in the midst of a great war, or ask reassignment. The latter would have involved demotion, for there was no other vice admiral's billet in the Bureau of Medicine and Surgery.

It is hardly necessary to add that McIntire's behavior after the war, affirming his wartime statements about the president's health, was all of a piece with the position the president would have asked him to take. It is possible that when the admiral engaged Creel to write *White House Physician* he found himself in an awkward place where he could hardly give Creel much to write about. Creel, to be sure, was vastly unhappy with the restatements but proved willing to repeat them. In 1951 when Farley made his remarks about Roosevelt's health, McIntire would have done better to remain silent, but having written a protesting letter to the *Washington Star* he went ahead and doubled his error by making his points in *U.S. News and World Report.*

The president had no problem arranging for McIntire's silence, but could not have been sure of Bruenn, who unlike McIntire was not a regular navy officer and unlike McIntire had a professional reputation. This may explain Roosevelt's offhandedness with Bruenn— why he said nothing about the latter's medical specialty, why he never asked about blood pressure readings. He was devious in this regard, talking with Bruenn about all sorts of things, seeing him several times daily, with blood pressure readings each time, never saying anything about Bruenn's professional association in New York and, especially, not inquiring about the readings, resorting instead to readings by Commander Fox, about which he never informed Bruenn. He talked them over with Daisy, who was harmless politically, but to have spoken with Bruenn about the doctor's experiences in New York and in particular about the blood pressures would have shown concern for a condition he did not want recognized.

Roosevelt's treatment of Bruenn recalls a comment by Rosenman of how the president dealt with White House staff members and other subordinates, never telling them more than he had to.[1] It was an arrangement that irritated the president's special counsel who had seen a great deal of the president over many years and felt that such a procedure was terribly inefficient. FDR "seemed to delight in having two or more people do different but related parts of a single job which could better have been done by one person." He thought that "the Boss" loved secrecy, and although Roosevelt could not have explained such a modus operandi, if called upon, it was his favorite course in matters large and small. The president thereby obtained a sense of power, which he loved: he was "the only person who knew everything about a project." In Rosenman's case the president did this sort of thing to him in July 1944, and Rosenman found out about it when Roosevelt slipped up later on. Just before leaving Washington for Hyde Park and Chicago on the trip to San Diego and Hawaii, the president sent a letter to the Republican presidential candidate of 1940, Willkie, in an effort to contain Willkie during the forthcoming presidential election. There can be no question that this is what he was doing. On December 22, 1943, he had told Walker, "I ought to keep in the back of my mind that if they nominate Bricker or even Dewey we should try to get Willkie on our side. Said he would make a deal with him."[2] He engaged Rosenman for a preliminary effort, sending him to New York where he met Willkie in a suite at the St. Regis. Things were so hush-hush that when a waiter brought up some food, Willkie went into another room so the waiter would not see him. But when FDR sent the letter of July 13 he did not say a word to Rosenman about it. Six weeks later, after return from the Hawaiian trip, on which Rosenman accompanied the president, Roosevelt held a press conference, during which a reporter inquired if he, the president, had been in touch with Willkie. The president denied he was in touch. He then had to send another letter to Willkie explaining that for a moment he forgot he wrote the initial letter. Willkie and his friends were furious about this double-dealing, for it gave the appearance that Willkie was soliciting Roosevelt. Word of the letters got into the newspapers, and Rosenman thereupon discovered FDR had been withholding information from him, the president's own special counsel. After the president's death Rosenman wrote with wry amusement that members of the late president's staff were publishing conflicting accounts of how they had been at the center of this or that, when to Rosenman's own knowledge the president had dealt as partially with them as he had with him.

Beyond taking care of McIntire and Bruenn, the president would have hoped to ensure the silence of other physicians. He did not trust doctors, as he revealed in a story Eisenhower liked to tell. The general in January 1944 related a complaint by Lord Moran that Churchill when ill would take the thermometer out of his mouth and tell Moran his temperature. "I always do that," the prime minister explained to the American general. "I believe these doctors are trying to keep me in bed." Eisenhower told the story to Roosevelt. The president responded to Eisenhower, "Oh, that's nothing new. I've been doing that for years. I don't trust those fellows, either."[3] When Breckinridge Long at the State Department came up with gossip that physicians at Bethesda and the Mayo Clinic were speculating about Roosevelt's illness, with appalling accuracy, it must have seemed a godsend that Long told Steve Early, who either on his own or the president's authority called in the FBI. Apprised of the need for an investigation, Director Hoover moved immediately. He was a well-known busybody concerning government secrets, who fortified his own position by picking up gossip of all sorts, and would have enjoyed doing the White House a good turn, scaring physicians. Early gave the resultant report to McIntire, and it is difficult not to believe that one of them told the president about the harassment by Hoover's agents, although they would not have called it that.[4]

Several reasons might explain the president's secrecy over his illness in 1944–1945. One was that he always had been very much a self-contained person who confided in no one, and kept to his own ways. Frank Walker sensed this quality from visiting at Hyde Park where even the president's mother, to whom the son was obviously dutiful, seemed not quite able to "get to" him—there was a carefulness between the two, Walker believed, that avoided the usual intimacy of a mother-son relationship. Walker believed that the president from his earliest days, some time in his youthful years, learned to rely upon himself and no one else. It was a quality Walker often saw when the president received visitors in the executive offices of the White House or upstairs in the oval room, for the visitors would hear the Rooseveltian words, that the president was delighted, agreed absolutely, and would depart convinced of an intimacy that never existed.

The president's daughter, Anna, who knew him as well as anyone, perhaps better, agreed with Walker about the remarkable way in which her father kept things to himself. She told a friend, who told Vice President Wallace, who thought so much about the remark he put it in his diary shortly after the president had denied him renomination in 1944, that "He doesn't know any man and no man knows him. Even his own family doesn't know anything about him . . ." In an oral history made a few years before her death in 1975, Anna repeated this commentary by relating how her father failed to confide in her even when he was at Warm Springs for the last time, his life ebbing away. During that visit Anna had remained in Washington, caring for her young son who was seriously ill. "He used to call me every night on the phone to find out how Johnny was," she remembered. "He called me the night before, and he was just fine. He told me all about the barbecue that they were going to have the next day, and everything else. But there was a funny little thing there, just to show that he never discussed his real personal life with anyone, as we all know from reading the books—Lucy Mercer was also at Warm Springs. Now, as I said, I talked to Father every single evening, before he died, from the time he went down there. He called me. He never once mentioned Lucy Mercer."[5]

The quality of being self-contained may have verged on something else that like self-reliance would have explained the presidential secrecy. Roosevelt's two presidential successors agreed on the existence of this trait. President Truman never forgot what Roosevelt's leadership during the Great Depression meant for millions of near destitute or destitute—the times were that bad—Americans. The depression leadership may well, Truman often observed, have saved the country. The nation's thirty-third president also respected his predecessor's leadership during World War II when FDR had taken a confused country closer and closer to supporting Great Britain and the Soviet Union, and Pearl Harbor at last galvanized the nation, bringing the unity that even Roosevelt's leadership had been unable to achieve. But Truman despite his respect and admiration did not like Roosevelt, and the reason—Truman kept it well hidden—was that he believed Roosevelt "an awful egotist." Truman knew this from bitter experience; it was no theory. He had voted for every New Deal measure, including reorganization (which meant what the critics said: packing) of the Supreme Court. His reward was that in a three-cornered primary race for reelection in Missouri in 1940, with his principal opponent the destroyer of the Pendergast political machine in Kansas City, Gov. Lloyd C. Stark, the most difficult campaign of Truman's political life, more difficult than the presidential election of 1948, Roosevelt intrigued against Truman because he thought Stark would be the winner, and he wanted Missouri's electoral votes in his own third-term election to the presidency.

One might argue that Truman's irritation because of the president's failure to support him in the 1940 primary was not so much a sign of Roosevelt's egotism as Truman's. That after all, politics is a cutthroat business and there was no special reason why FDR should have supported a one-term senator during the senator's bid for a second term. That the president had every reason to consult his own needs, and whatever happened to Truman was a footnote. Truman knew this, and never lost his respect for Roosevelt's extraordinary political judgment, the president's ability to measure a situation coldly and make a rational solution—rationality being defined in terms of what suited the president. The man of Independence, unlike his wife (who disliked Roosevelt thereafter with an ill-concealed disdain), knew a pro when he saw one. Nonetheless, the best of politics must be defined not merely in terms of self-interest but in terms of a sort of noble charity, willingness to stick by friends, some tincture of loyalty. Truman grew up in Jackson County, Missouri, where loyalty in politics was something everyone expected. It was the cement of the party, absolutely necessary, so his friends said. He felt that way, and when he became president he sometimes showed what seemed an absurd loyalty. While he understood, thoroughly understood, Roosevelt's motive or motives for supporting Governor Stark during the primary, he did not think it a lovely attribute of the president's, and never forgot it, even though he expressed for it less venom than did his more emotional wife, who was close to being a Roosevelt hater.

President Eisenhower favored the election of Roosevelt in 1932, and if his Republican instincts reasserted themselves was nonetheless indebted to FDR for wartime preferment to high command. He was the direct choice of General Marshall for command in England in 1942. But thereafter a problem arose, a most difficult one for "Ike," because the choice of a commander for the invasion of France in 1944 was essentially between Marshall and Eisenhower. Neither was pushing against the other. During the North African campaign and the opening of the Italian campaign, months went by without a decision. Eisenhower was reduced to making roundabout inquiries of Elliott Roosevelt. After a very considerable delay, which Eisenhower seems to have blamed upon the president, the choice was made. Perhaps also the Allies' supreme European commander received too many presidential military judgments, occasionally offered. Like Truman he was careful in making his dislike known; there was no large reason to remark it, and Eisenhower was a cautious man and did not do so. During his presidential administration he sometimes used a recording system in his office, recording important conversations and allowing the recordings to be typed up. Some were not. A recording, never typed, was discovered and released in 1997 that caught the Republican president referring to Roosevelt, remarking that he was "almost an egomaniac in his beliefs, in his own wisdom."[6]

If the president's self-contained, his successors would have said egotistical, ways constituted one reason Roosevelt revealed no more than was necessary about his illness in 1944–1945, another might have been that the presidency was convenient to him. Although he lived nicely at Hyde Park, which was an estate and not a farm (the president on occasion described it as a farm, and himself a farmer), he was not really a rich man; the Roosevelt income had derived from the China trade of a century before, and there was not all that much of it, and the president had put most of his personal funds into Warm Springs. The office of president was convenient, for everything was paid for, transportation and lodging and food. He also enjoyed the ceremonial of being president. He was "Mr. President." No one save Louis Howe, FDR's closest adviser, who died in 1936, and his mother, who passed on in 1941, and his wife, to be sure, used *his* first name. He called other people by their first names.[7] Only General Marshall refused such an appellation. The book by Bishop about Roosevelt's last year sought to make a point that Roosevelt grew tired of the rigmarole, of listening to "Hail to the Chief." There is no evidence of that. Behind the ceremonial was the power; the ceremonial announced it. Roosevelt never complained in any convincing way that the office of president was a bother. Moreover, he had nothing to go back to. His marriage had lapsed. His children, save Anna, had gone their own ways. His life was politics. In the early 1920s he suffered from the loneliness of his then illness, and it was the reappearance of politics, which his for once understanding wife brought back to him through visits of politically inclined people and he continued through correspondence, that saved him. Roosevelt could speak to Mackenzie King about writing a newspaper column after he retired from the presidency in 1949, but that would have been a pallid experience after holding the presidency. Bob Nixon, the White House reporter who saw a great deal of Roosevelt, thought the president was planning to take a fifth term. If he had trouble with Congress after the Supreme Court fight he was invincible in national elections, the best campaigner since Andrew Jackson.[8]

Another reason for secrecy is worth mentioning, although it is difficult to be sure of. This was Roosevelt's behavior about his poliomyelitis. He did everything possible to cover it up. When talking with people he would be seated in an ordinary chair. If giving a speech he arranged to have his wheelchair pushed up a ramp surrounded with Secret Service men until he was on the podium and could lock in his braces and an assistant could pull him up erect. If possible he spoke from an automobile. It was well known that photographers could not photograph the president in a wheelchair, and anyone who sought to do so might find his camera taken by a Secret Service man and his film exposed. In the Roosevelt Library collection of thirty-five thousand still photographs, until quite recently there were only two showing the president in a wheelchair and no newsreels showing him lifted, carried, or pushed. Many of his fellow Americans did not know that the president was incapable of walking unaided, save for leaning unsteadily on two canes, and that when standing he had to grasp a lectern or hold onto the arm of an assistant. Virtually denying that he used a wheelchair, he would have had no large task denying his cardiovascular disease.

One cannot be certain that one successful denial produced another. In Roosevelt's time people afflicted with deafness or blindness or, in his case, polio often were considered different from other individuals, and treated with pity rather than supported for their essential humanity. It was probably politically wise for FDR to hide his physical disability.

It is possible to draw too much from Roosevelt's bout with polio. Wheelchair users undoubtedly experience the world differently. They see people standing while they are seated. They wheel themselves to places, day after day, year after year, or someone carries them. They receive gentle explanations of sympathy, constantly reminded of a life that is not like that of other people. The experience can bring an understanding of reality that is different, in which the word *survival* has daily meaning. But the recent president of the College of Physicians of Philadelphia, Dr. Alfred P. Fishman, rightly has pointed out that life in a wheelchair affects different individuals in different ways. Some wheelchair occupants are largely unaffected. For them, patterns of behavior have been set by other experiences. Had they possessed full use of their extremities they would have acted in the same ways.[9]

In Roosevelt's decision to disguise his illness there was little or no participation by his family, which as Early said for the most part ignored him, apart from using him. His wife sought to help but was incapable of it. Anna could deal with him easier than any other member of the family, but he did not take her into his confidence. A quarter century after his death she asked Dr. Bruenn if he thought McIntire told her father the real cause of his illness. She told the journalist Richard Rovere she believed her father had no idea why he was going down so rapidly, what his trouble was.[10]

The cost to the Republic was surely great. Roosevelt in his last year was arguably as incapacitated as President Wilson had been, a shell of his former self, unable to keep abreast of the great decisions he had left to the end of the war, too ill or too arrogant to inform his successor about them.[11]

Had Roosevelt been a well man, the Honolulu Conference over strategy in the Far East might have gone far differently. At issue was the U.S. Navy's strategy of a move across the Pacific, westward to the Japanese home islands, by way of Formosa, versus the U.S. Army's strategy of island-hopping north from Australia, via the Philippines and Okinawa. General MacArthur had a personal stake in invasion of the Philippines, for he had spent half a dozen years, beginning in 1935, attempting to create a Philippine army that despite reinforcement with thousands of Americans had collapsed within a few months, giving the islands to the rapacious Japanese. He had said that he would return. Upon his troops' return in 1944 he underestimated the Japanese defenses, and the campaign took longer and was far more costly than he anticipated. It included the building-by-building conquest of Manila. The subsequent Okinawa campaign resulted in more delay, with ferocious Japanese resistance and very high casualties. Conquest of the Philippines and Okinawa created a timetable for invasion of the Japanese home islands that placed the proposed invasion of the southernmost home island, Kyushu, just before the winter months of 1945. The prospect of invading Kyushu and subsequently Honshu (the Tokyo plain) planned for April 1946 made the nuclear bombing of Japan attractive. There is little evidence that these subjects had the analysis they deserved at the Honolulu Conference. In any event a two-hour meeting was a ridiculous amount of time for them. One wonders whether the strategy advocated by Adm. Chester W. Nimitz, a thrust into Formosa instead of the Philippines and Okinawa, might have been a quicker and far less costly course.

The conferees at Hawaii could have confronted the increasing rottenness of the Chiang Kai-shek regime in China. In the crucial summer of 1944 the president chose to avoid that issue, and replaced Gen. Joseph W. Stilwell by a junior commander, Lt. Gen. Albert C. Wedemeyer, who went along with the Chiang policy of doing little or nothing in the war against Japan. Making matters worse, FDR allowed one of his favorites, the erstwhile Oklahoma oil wildcatter and President Herbert Hoover's secretary of war, Patrick

J. Hurley, an ignoramus on matters Chinese, to become his personal representative to the Chiang government. On the eve of his final journey to Warm Springs a weary FDR gave Hurley what he wanted: unqualified backing for Chiang's regime. If Roosevelt had proposed a different course in China he might have saved his successor as president the debacle of the Communist takeover in 1949, and with it the subsequent Korean War.

A more alert President Roosevelt might have prevented the debacle of the Vietnam War a generation later, and all it meant for the reputation of the American military (resounding defeat) and for American politics (the resignation of President Richard M. Nixon, because military deceptions over Vietnam encouraged political deceptions). During World War II, Roosevelt had not hesitated to take anti-imperial positions, notably against British rule in India. He seemed ready to do the same for French return to Indochina. In the event he failed to make allowance for the nationalist movement in Indochina under Ho Chi Minh, and the French returned, failed, and the Americans sought to take over.

For Europe, President Roosevelt displayed such appalling judgment as to sponsor the Morgenthau Plan, which would have created a postwar German nation of farmers; it was a plan to destroy the industrial heart of Europe. Roosevelt and Churchill initialed this proposal at the Quebec Conference in September 1944. It would have destroyed Western civilization in countries where it had flourished for centuries. Secretary of War Stimson and Secretary of State Hull immediately opposed the foolish, suicidal plan, and within weeks it disappeared, as quickly as it had arisen. The bewildered FDR asserted that he had no such plan, was "frankly staggered . . . and said he had no idea how he could have initiated this."[12] It is clear that only an ill president, and a prime minister whose nation needed the postwar financial support that an American secretary of the treasury could provide, would have advanced such a scheme.

The president remarked his concern over the Holocaust in a few wartime pronouncements, but surely could have done more than that. Perhaps more warnings of Judgment Day to the Nazi leadership would have accomplished little, given Adolf Hitler's inflexible will to destroy the Jewish people. Auschwitz was photographed in 1944, and a nearby industrial target was bombed. The Auschwitz photographs were not recognized for what they were, perhaps because of inability during World War II to enlarge photographs more than seven times. The negatives were not interpreted until 1979. With the magnification then possible they showed the camp's terrible purpose, its gas chambers and crematoria. It is probable that bombing the railroad lines from Hungary to Auschwitz would have been ineffective in saving the lives of the 340,000 Hungarian Jews who went to their deaths in 1944; there were too many rail lines, and their repair would have been a matter of a few days. Yet, could not the U.S. Army Air Forces and the Royal Air Force have roused themselves (with presidential encouragement) to make an effort? And could not American and British planes have dropped leaflets incessantly on German cities, the American and British governments appealed publicly and constantly to the Vatican, their information services spread the message of the Holocaust by every possible means? If ineffective in saving lives, such measures would have been better than the policy followed, which in large part awaited the overrunning of the camps in 1945.

The truth is that during World War II the Roosevelt administration did not respond well to the near annihilation of European Jewry. Admittedly, discrimination against Germany's Jews did not reach fever pitch until the pogrom of 1938, known as *Kristallnacht*, the night of destruction of the windows and looting of Jewish shops and the burning of synagogues. The president largely through Undersecy. of State Sumner Welles interpreted the requirement that immigrants not be "public charges" liberally. But with the beginning of the war and the fall of France in 1940, FDR succumbed to the "fifth column" myth, fear that Germany would commingle spies with the refugees, and told the Department of State to administer refugee cases narrowly. Rescue became a marginal issue. Welles did not really challenge existing procedures until after his ouster from the State Department in 1943. Secretary Hull hesitated to involve himself because his wife was Jewish and he did not want anyone to accuse him of a personal policy. When Secretary Morgenthau forced the issue into the open in 1944, which led to the creation of the War Refugee Board, President Roosevelt was deathly ill and hardly possessed the energy to oppose the Holocaust in the way he might have, with every exertion his administration could make, physically and through spreading the word.

The president's choice of Truman as a running mate in 1944 rested on maneuvering by party leaders, rather than his own judgment, and displayed his thoughtlessness about his illness. He was willing to advise Vice President Wallace to seek a second term, a dangerous proposition considering Wallace's desire to push the issue, for the then vice president knew well what was at stake. The president's willingness to allow Byrnes to make a try for the nomination was equally dangerous. As for what he had in mind for Truman, it is clear that he believed he would live out his fourth term or do even better. If he told Daisy Suckley he might resign after the war, it was unbelievable, for by his own admission in midsummer 1944 he hardly knew Truman and thereafter made little effort to know him. He would never, one must believe, have passed the presidency to Truman.

After allowing the designation of Truman as his running mate, Roosevelt failed to inform his successor of anything, military, diplomatic, or administrative, save one casual admission about the atomic bomb. It was an invitation to national calamity. He chose to say nothing about the agreement with Churchill over postwar nuclear sharing concluded at Hyde Park on September 18, 1944, and demonstrated a worse lapse by not informing the State Department. His failure to discuss Yalta with his vice president was all of a piece with his belief that Truman was an inconsequential member of the administration. He compounded these errors by telling Truman nothing about the mechanism of the American government, the responsibility for which Truman inherited just before the country underwent a complicated conversion from a wartime to a peacetime economy and when he was dealing with an increasingly hostile Soviet Union. It was a time when the government needed to function at its best, and Truman knew so little about the mechanism that it sometimes functioned at its worst. The man from Missouri was an admirable substitute for what death had taken, and in time Truman used organization charts and used good men wisely. But he inherited jerry-rigged relationships that he hardly knew. Government under Roosevelt was so personal that only the nation's chief executive knew how it worked; Truman needed tutelage on how to deal with different constituencies and different advocates. Roosevelt had created a Rube Goldberg machine and did not give Truman an operator's manual. Or if the nation's chief executive during the Great Depression and World War II was a juggler, he did not tell Truman how many balls were in the air, nor mention how to keep them aloft. If FDR was a puppeteer, he had let the strings go, and Truman did not know how to retrieve them. Sometimes Truman may have been tempted to believe that Roosevelt was the Wizard of Oz; Truman knew Kansas, almost as well as Missouri, and would have been tempted to think that FDR's act was so much hot air, that he, Truman, was only the new Wizard.

All in all, Roosevelt's physical decline meant that he removed himself from government, that policy was being made without his making the big decisions, that momentum and bureaucratic battles determined final outcomes. The president knew he was ill, even if he had delusions of immortality. In his illness, his utter weariness, with a feeling that he knew best, he engaged in denials that came to appear as affirmations. They were attractive, and made sense as far as they went, which was not very far.

▪ *President Roosevelt's*
Blood Pressures

Sources:

a = "Roosevelt, Franklin D.: Medical Blood Pressure Statistics, 1935–1944," and "Franklin D. Roosevelt: Medical, Special Examination . . . ," box 66, Anna Roosevelt Halsted papers

b = Bruenn Diary

c = Kenneth R. Crispell and Carlos F. Gomez, *Hidden Illness in the White House*, 192

d = Geoffrey C. Ward, ed., *Closest Companion: The Unknown Story of the Intimate Friendship between Franklin Roosevelt and Margaret Suckley*, 380

April 29, 1931	140/100	c
July 30, 1935	136/78	a
April 22, 1937	162/98	a
November 13, 1940	178/88	a
February 27, 1941	188/105; 178/102	a
May 5, 1941 6:35 p.m.,	148/80	a
May 6 (?), 1941 10:45 p.m.,	152/86	a
May 7 (?), 1941 9:15 a.m.,	162/84	a
May 8 (?), 1941 4:10 p.m.,	148/80	a
May 9 (?), 1941 6:15 p.m.,	156/86	a
May 10 (?), 1941 10:15 p.m.,	146/82	a
March 27 (28), 1944	186/108	b
March 28, 1944	180/90; 170/110	b
March 29, 1944	184/108; 186/108	a; b
March 30, 1944	180/104	b
March 31, 1944	220-230/120-130;	
	11:00 a.m., 202/110	b

April 1, 1944	192-200/106-108	b
April 3, 1944	208-210/108-110	b
April 4, 1944	222-226/118	b
April 5, 1944	218/120	b
April 6, 1944	210/120	b
April 7, 1944	208/114	b
April 9, 1944	202/102; p.m., 198/98	a
April 10, 1944	196/94; p.m., 200/104	a
April 11, 1944	192/96; p.m., 204/100	a
April 12, 1944	200/102; p.m., 204/98	a
April 13, 1944	198/100; p.m., 202/98	a
April 14, 1944	206/100; p.m., 200/96	a
April 15, 1944	208/102; p.m., 196/100	a
April 16, 1944	215/102; p.m., 206/120	a
April 17, 1944	216/120; p.m., 206/116	a
April 18, 1944	220/120	a
April 19, 1944	218/120; p.m., 204/104	a
April 19–20, 1944	230/126-128 (before breakfast)	
	210/106 (hour later)	
	218/112 (five minutes later)	
	190/90 (evening)	b
April 20, 1944	212/108	
	noon, 210/98	
	9:54 p.m., 190/100	a
April 21, 1944	9:05 a.m., 234/126	
	10:00 a.m. (sitting), 210/116	
	10:05 a.m. (supine, both arms ejected), 218/120	
	6:45 p.m. (after resting), 214/120	
	9:50 p.m., 220/114	a
April 21, 1944	234/126; 210/114	b
April 22, 1944	9:30 a.m., 214/120	
	11:30 a.m., 210/114	
	6:30 p.m. (after boat trip), 208/110	a
April 23, 1944	10:15 a.m. (2.5-hour drive), 214/118	
	9:45 p.m., 212/114	a
April 24, 1944	10:00 a.m., 222/122	
	10:30 p.m., 220/116	a

April 25, 1944	10:05 a.m., 224/116
	1:00 p.m. (after luncheon party), a 214/106
April 26, 1944	10:00 a.m., 214/112
	10:30 p.m., 222/110 a
April 27, 1944	10:15 a.m., 222/118
	9:45 p.m., 210/114 a
April 28, 1944	224/124; p.m., 230/120 a
April 29, 1944	9:00 (on awaking), 196/112
	10:10 (sitting after breakfast), 236/120
	(supine, after EKG), 220/118
	2:15 (after lunch), 236/112
	9:30 p.m., 210/110 a
April 30, 1944	8:45 (supine, on awaking), 210/110
	10:00 (after breakfast), 208/104
	(after lunch), 208/114
	9:00 p.m., 234/120 a
May 1, 1944	9:00 a.m. (supine), 220/116
	noon, 210/110
	2:00 (after lunch), 210/106
	1:30 p.m., 210/112 a
May 2, 1944	9:00 a.m., 216/116
	10:00 a.m., 226/112
	10:30 p.m., 240/130 a
May 3, 1944	10:00 a.m., 210/118
	9:00 p.m., 220/120 a
May 4, 1944	9:00 a.m., 218/120
	(EKG) 210/116
	9:30 p.m., 216/118 a
May 5, 1944	9:00 a.m., 210/108
	9:50 p.m., 202/104 a
May 6, 1944	9:30 a.m., 206/106 a
May 8, 1944	10:10 a.m., 204/118 a
May 9, 1944	10:05 a.m., 208/114 a
May 10, 1944	9:50 a.m. (EKG), 206/110 a
May 11, 1944	10:10 a.m., 210/106 a
June 1, 1944	9:50 a.m., 206/108

	7:20 p.m., 184/96	a
June 2, 1944	10:00 a.m., 220/106	
	10:20 p.m., 198/98	a
June 3, 1944	10:15 a.m., 206/110	
	9:50 p.m., 188/88	a
June 4, 1944	9:50 a.m., 198/100	
	10:55 p.m., 186/94	a
June 5, 1944	9:35 a.m., 194/98	a
June 6, 1944	10:15 a.m., 210/122	a
June 7, 1944	9:45 (before breakfast), 208/110	a
June 8, 1944	10:50 a.m., 220/128	a
June 9, 1944	9:45 a.m., 208/104	a
June 10, 1944	9:45 (before breakfast), 202/104	a
June 11, 1944	10:15 a.m., 212/114	a
June 12, 1944	9:40 a.m., 210/120	a
June 13, 1944	9:10 a.m., 200/106	
	6:50 p.m., 194/96	a
June 14, 1944	9:50 a.m., 216/118	a
September 15, 1944	240/130	b
September 20, 1944	past few weeks, from 180/100	b
November 18, 1944	210/112	b
December 6, 1944	260/150	b
January 12, 1945	190/88 (98?)	d
February 16, 1945	blood pressure at usual levels	b
February 21, 1945	blood pressure quite variable over the past few days	b
March 28, 1945	blood pressure values somewhat lower	b
April 6, 1945	blood pressure levels as before, extremely wide, 170/88 to 240/130	b
April 12, 1945	blood pressure systolic well over 300, diastolic 190	
	2:45 p.m., 240/120	
	3:15 p.m., 210/110	b

▪ *Notes*

Chapter 1: Guesswork

1. Ross T. McIntire, *White House Physician*, 206.

2. Ibid., 14–15, 206.

3. *New York Times,* August 9, 1956, "Roosevelt, Franklin D.–health," vertical file, Franklin D. Roosevelt Library. The vertical file is a catchall of newspaper clippings and popular and scholarly articles, filed by topic, housed in filing cases.

4. On the second day of Roosevelt's illness he lost the ability to move his legs. Keen saw him on the third day and concluded "that a clot of blood from a sudden congestion has settled in the lower spinal cord temporarily removing the power to move though not to feel." He prescribed massage and predicted that recovery might "take some months." As Roosevelt's condition worsened in the next days Keen altered his diagnosis from a clot to a lesion in the spinal cord (James R. Roosevelt to FDR, August 18, 1921, in Elliott Roosevelt, ed., *F.D.R.: His Personal Letters,* 2:523–25).

5. McIntire, *White House Physician,* 54. The Northampton resident, a former newspaperman turned freelance writer, Earle Looker, published his account in "Is Franklin D. Roosevelt Physically Fit to Be President?"

6. McIntire, *White House Physician,* 67.

7. A dramatic exposé, the Flexner Report by Abraham Flexner and N. P. Colwell, the latter secretary of the council on medical education of the American Medical Association, brought to public attention the many diploma-mill schools of medicine in the United States and Canada. The schools were both proprietary and university related. Of 165 medical schools in 1900, fewer than 70 remained within a few years after the report. The latter required two years of preprofessional college education and a four-year graded curriculum, together with an approved internship. Medical schools had to maintain a substantial full-time clinical faculty. Not long thereafter residencies were established, although not required. In 1917 the AMA inaugurated specialty examining boards.

8. McIntire, *White House Physician,* 56.

9. Ibid., 57–58.

10. Bert E. Park, *The Impact of Illness on World Leaders*, 7, 35–36, 230–31.

11. McIntire, *White House Physician*, 58, 63–64.

12. Ibid., 139.

13. Ibid., 19, 180, 194.

14. Admiral McIntire's remarks were published in the *New York Times*; William D. Hassett, *Off the Record with F.D.R.: 1942–1945*, 250; McIntire, *White House Physician*, 17.

15. Thomas M. Campbell and George C. Herring, eds., *The Diaries of Edward R. Stettinius, Jr.: 1943–1946*, 316; Joseph E. Davies Diary, April 12; Harold L. Ickes Diary, August 26, 1945.

16. Memorandum of April 29, 1946, "White House Physician," box 12, Ross T. McIntire Papers.

17. Creel to McIntire, June 7, 1946, "White House Physician," box 12, McIntire Papers.

18. The book was a modest success financially. The admiral and Creel shared equally in royalties. The first printing was fifteen thousand copies, and Putnam's expected that a second printing of three thousand would supply demand for several months. After an advance of $1,000 McIntire received a first-year royalty of $1,012.48 (Kennett L. Rawson to Clare R. Murphy, secretary to Admiral McIntire, February 12, 1947, "White House Physician," box 12, McIntire Papers).

19. Charles E. Bohlen, *Witness to History: 1929–1969*, 143–44.

20. Comment by Dr. Robert Bradley at a lecture by the author, "The Illness and Death of Franklin D. Roosevelt," College of Physicians of Philadelphia, October 30, 1996.

21. The following is from Dr. Harry S. Goldsmith's "Unanswered Mysteries in the Death of Franklin D. Roosevelt"; telephone conversation with Dr. Goldsmith, December 26, 1996; *New York Times*, October 15, 1985, February 19, 1986; Herbert Dan Adams, *The Knife That Saves: Memoirs of a Lahey Clinic Surgeon*, 217–19.

22. Dr. Samuel Day of Jacksonville, Florida, former president of the Florida Medical Association, related another version of the story offered by Dr. Pack, who visited Day in the late 1950s and again in 1965. "One night," Day wrote, "he related a story, which had been told to him by Dr. Frank Lahey. It seems that President Roosevelt and his entourage came to Boston by special train to see Dr. Lahey prior to his final race for reelection in 1944. After intensive studies at the Lahey Clinic it was found that he had advanced cancer of the stomach. I am sure that was the stated site, as I was surprised at never having heard of any of FDR's 'stomach ailments' before that. Dr. Lahey told Dr. Pack that he related the findings to the president and told him he was a very sick man and he could not advise him to run for

office again. Mr. Roosevelt was said to have replied, 'Well, I *am* running,' to which Dr. Lahey replied, 'Well, Mr. President, I would suggest that you take on a strong vice president' " (Jack Anderson and Joseph Spear, "Evidence Indicates FDR Knew of Cancer," *Washington Post*, July 2, 1987, "Roosevelt, Franklin D.–health," vertical file).

23. My colleague in the history of medicine at Indiana University, Ann Carmichael, M.D., called this lecture, "The Last Illness of Franklin D. Roosevelt," to my attention, as she attended the conference and heard it. Inquiry to Dr. Hudson for a copy of the paper revealed that he had spoken from notes. An unidentified AP article of May 7, 1986, reporting the lecture of May 1, is in "Roosevelt, Franklin D.–health," vertical file.

24. Hugh L'Etang is the author of, among other works, *Fit to Lead?* (London: Heinemann, 1980) and *Ailing Leaders in Power: 1914–1994* (London: Royal Society of Medicine Books, 1995). *The Pathology of Leadership* cites *Modern Medicine* (March 6, 1961): 211. The paper before the American Surgical Association in St. Louis, April 20, 1949, was published by William S. McCune, "Malignant Melanoma: Forty Cases Treated by Radical Resection." It contained a photograph of the malignant melanoma of the brain (320) with the date "A-14–45," and did not comment upon it in the eight cases discussed.

25. According to McIntire, Lahey and Paullin saw Roosevelt late in May 1944 (*White House Physician*, 187). Paullin's daughter told Dr. Hugh E. Evans that Paullin discussed his White House trips with no one, nor left memoranda, diaries, notes, or medical records ("The Medical History of President Franklin D. Roosevelt," 59). Dr. Howard G. Bruenn's article is "Clinical Notes on the Illness and Death of President Franklin D. Roosevelt."

26. Evans, "Medical History of President Roosevelt," 111 n; Brenda L. Heaster interview with Dr. Bruenn, April 21–22, 1989, 8–9; I am indebted to an associate of Craig at the Mayo Clinic, Dr. David C. Voris, presently of Hanover, Indiana, for identifying Craig's connection with Roosevelt.

27. Geoffrey C. Ward, ed., *Closest Companion: The Unknown Story of the Intimate Friendship between Franklin Roosevelt and Margaret Suckley,* 275.

28. Ibid., 277. "But actually, I don't know why I should talk about this, it's merely—it might be called a—a preventive—and that is very often necessary, to use a preventive—I had a pain for—I don't know, what?— twenty years or less; and I don't know, what you call a wen on the back of my head. And it had grown a bit lately, so I went out to the Naval Hospital, and two very good surgeons, and knives, and God knows what, removed it under a local anesthetic. I think I was in the hospital half an hour. So now she's out" (*Complete Presidential Press Conferences of Franklin D. Roosevelt*, 23:20).

29. Edward J. Flynn, *You're the Boss*, 217.

30. Ward, *Closest Companion*, 278, 280.

Chapter 2: March 28, 1944

1. Ibid., 249; Lord Moran (Charles Wilson), *Churchill: Taken from the Diaries of Lord Moran: The Struggle for Survival, 1940–1965*, 103; on Churchill's annoyance with questions by his physician early in mornings, see Sir John R. Colville, "The Personality of Sir Winston Churchill," 120–21.

2. Ward, *Closest Companion*, 249–50.

3. Ibid., 250.

4. Ibid., 252.

5. Suckley Diary, January 1, 1944, microfilm, Franklin D. Roosevelt Library; Harold D. Smith Diary, "Conferences with President Roosevelt, 1943–1945," January 7, 1944, Smith Papers.

6. Suckley Diary, January 18, 1944, microfilm.

7. Hassett, *Off the Record*, 233.

8. Ward, *Closest Companion*, 278.

9. Loc. cit.

10. Ibid., 285.

11. Ibid., 282–83.

12. Ickes Diary, December 27, 1947; Norman M. Littell, *My Roosevelt Years*, 74.

13. Hassett, *Off the Record*, 238; Ward, *Closest Companion*, 281.

14. Suckley Diary, March 19, 20, 23, microfilm.

15. Hassett, *Off the Record*, 239.

16. Ickes Diary, July 16, 1948.

17. The typescript version of the Bruenn diary gives the proper date and shows two other blood pressures, 180/90 and 170/110.

18. Jan Kenneth Herman, "The President's Cardiologist," 9; author's interview, February 16, 1992.

19. "Had a very good trip. Went to a very great many places where there are American troops—sailors, and so forth. Done at my request, as you probably know. Apparently did a lot of good" (*Presidential Press Conferences*, 23:120–21).

20. Ward, *Closest Companion*, 288.

21. *New York Times*, March 31, April 5, 1944.

22. Bruenn Diary, March 28, 1944.

23. Herman, "The President's Cardiologist," 8.

24. Brenda L. Heaster, interview, 33.

25. Ibid., 41. Paullin especially irritated Bruenn. Paullin's mushy opinions were evident in a letter of May 25, 1951, to Albert S. McCowen,

concerning the president's illness: "Essential hypertension with arteriosclerosis. The hypertension was variable. He had some EKG evidence of coronary artery disease, and some evidence of cardiac enlargement" (Kenneth R. Crispell and Carlos F. Gomez, *Hidden Illness in the White House*, 140).

26. Bruenn, "Clinical Notes," 581.

27. Heaster, interview, 41.

28. Herman, "The President's Cardiologist," 8.

29. Heaster, interview, 33.

30. Bruenn, "Clinical Notes."

31. Park, *Impact of Illness*, 248, 284.

32. Heaster, interview, 37.

33. Loc. cit.; Herman, "The President's Cardiologist," 13.

34. Herman, "The President's Cardiologist," 8; Anna Roosevelt Halsted to Bruenn, January 13, 1969, box 8, Anna Roosevelt Halsted Papers; Heaster, interview, 26–27.

Chapter 3: Getting Along

1. W. L. Mackenzie King Diary, September 11, 1944.

2. "Conferences with President Roosevelt, 1943–1945," box 3, Smith Papers.

3. Ward, *Closest Companion*, 291.

4. "Notes on President's Trip to Hobcaw," 13, "President's Trips— Memoranda re Arrangements," William M. Rigdon Papers.

5. Unlike preceding entries, Bruenn summarized this and the following in "Clinical Notes."

6. Ibid., 584.

7. Ward, *Closest Companion*, 295–96.

8. Ibid., 294–95.

9. Ibid., 296. Also December 29, 1944, January 2, 8, 1945, in ibid., 372, 377–78. For the contention over the diastolic pressure see January 12, in ibid., 380. There is one other possible way that the president might have learned about his problem. Some years after the president died, the neurosurgeon David Voris, then practicing in Chicago, spent three years at the Mayo Clinic and the department head was Winchell Craig, the surgeon who in February 1944 removed the wen from the back of the president's head and probably the sebaceous cyst over the president's left eyebrow. Craig told Dr. Voris and another physician that he had made an pneumoencephalogram of the president at the White House—to see if there was an intracranial disease, possibly a stroke. With the assistance of Dr. Voris the present writer sought to discover papers left by Craig, to no avail.

10. The president was "most jovial," and the consultants talked to him at least an hour (Paullin to McIntire, June 24, 1946, "White House Physician," box 12, McIntire Papers). The routine as decided on May 5, 1944, was 8:30 to 9:00 a.m., breakfast in quarters; 11:00 to 1:00 p.m., office; 1:00 to 2:00 p.m., luncheon in quarters, no business guests; 2:00 to 3:00 p.m., rest lying down; 3:00 to 5:00 p.m., office; forty-five minutes of massage and ultraviolet light, rest before dinner, lying down; 7:30 to 8:00 p.m., dinner in quarters, no night work, sleep ten hours ("Collier's Article . . . ," box 2, McIntire Papers).

11. Clipping in Suckley Diary, microfilm.

12. John T. Flynn, *The Roosevelt Myth,* 399; Crispell and Gomez, *Hidden Illness,* 83.

13. Jonathan Daniels, *White House Witness: 1942–1945,* 220. The George Fort Milton book was *The Use of Presidential Power: 1789–1943* (Boston: Little, Brown, 1944).

14. Ward, *Closest Companion,* 308, 312, 314.

15. Suckley Diary, May 22, 24, 25, 29, 30, 31, June 1, microfilm.

16. Dr. Robert Travis Canon had been a member of the navy medical corps in World War I, and was a reservist while pursuing a practice in Lubbock, Texas, until 1940, when he was recalled to active service. He was chief of the Eye, Ear, Nose, and Throat Department at the National Naval Medical Center at Bethesda, 1942–1944. At the end of the war he retired with the rank of commodore.

17. *New York Times,* August 9, 1956, "Roosevelt, Franklin D.–health," vertical file. When Mrs. Roosevelt related in 1956 that "the doctors" had said her husband was fit for a fourth term she spoke of a series of physical examinations in May 1944 and must have meant the gallbladder test upon return from South Carolina that involved Drs. Paullin and Lahey.

18. Frank Freidel, *Franklin D. Roosevelt: A Rendezvous with Destiny,* 513; conversation with Dr. Bruenn, February 16, 1992.

19. Michael F. Reilly, *Reilly of the White House.*

20. The importance of Roosevelt's illness in the decision to displace Wallace became known in 1950 when Jonathan Daniels published *The Man of Independence* (Philadelphia: Lippincott), an authorized biography of President Truman; he used a memorandum given him by Pauley. Mrs. Roosevelt evidently did not read the book and in 1956 told a reporter that her husband's health played no part in fourth-term decisions in 1944 (*New York Times,* August 9, 1956).

21. Ward, *Closest Companion,* 318.

22. Early to Tully, July 28, 1944, "Tully, Grace–memos," box 24, Stephen T. Early Papers.

23. Skadding to Early, August 2, 1944, "Pictures of the President—Good and Bad—used in 1944," box 33, Early Papers.

24. James Roosevelt and Sidney Shalett, *Affectionately, FDR: A Son's Story of a Courageous Man*, 351–52; James Roosevelt with Bill Libby, *My Parents: A Differing View*, x, 278–79.

25. The following account of the trip to Hawaii and the Aleutians is from the Bruenn Diary, July 26, 27, 28, 29, 30, August 3, 3–4, 5–6, 7.

26. The above, together with the following, is from the Bruenn Diary.

27. Grace Tully, *F.D.R., My Boss*, 278.

28. Herman, "The President's Cardiologist," 9.

29. McIntire, *White House Physician*, 202.

30. King Diary, September 10–11, 1944. On the next day, September 12, Churchill, the president, and Mackenzie King were looking at models of equipment that had been made for the Normandy invasion. "I noticed when Mrs. Roosevelt was wheeling the President's chair, and as he was looking at the models, that out of sheer weakness, there was perspiration on his forehead. While he looked better today than yesterday, he still looks very weak. I feel a great concern for him. She seemed anxious to get him off to bed for an afternoon rest." After bidding the president good-bye on September 16, King wrote, "He certainly has not the grasp today that he had a year ago. He looks very tired. I noticed in conversation after he sat down on the train, that the front of his face, forehead, nose and mouth—about a hand's breadth, became quite flushed. It was curious how this was in a line. He looked frail as he sat alone having gotten off his chair into the larger chair." Next day, September 17, King walked up and down the Citadel at Quebec and noticed the absence of the American flag on the pole. He "felt it to be a sort of ill omen as if the President might be the first to be taken of the three of us" (King Diary).

31. Howard G. Bruenn, interview.

32. The president's late time of retirement is in the Louise Hachmeister Diary, September 15, 1944. Hachmeister, present on the trip, was the White House telephone operator. Roosevelt's blood pressure had risen to the same figures on May 2, 1944, at the time of the second gallbladder attack at Hobcaw.

33. McIntire, *White House Physician*, 204.

34. The following is from J. Edgar Hoover to Stephen T. Early, November 1, 1944, enclosing "Memorandum re circulation of story alleging the president has a serious heart affliction, October 29, 1944," in "Roosevelt, Franklin D.: Correspondence and White House Matters," box 9, McIntire Papers.

35. To frequent observers the president often looked as good as he did

in the Tames photograph. One of his longtime assistants (she had come in at the beginning of the administration in 1933) in the White House offices, Lela Mae Stiles, attended the press conference on July 10, 1944, at which the president announced he was willing to accept nomination for a fourth term. She described it as "one of our most thrilling conferences." She wrote that she went up front, "as close to him as from our living room door to the door into the hall, or closer, I believe. I had just been reading one of the hellish anti-Roosevelt papers that talked and talked of his health, how old he was, etc. etc. and harped on the 'old in office' theme till I wanted to get another good look at him and Lordy, he looks grand! He was in shirt sleeves and had on a blue polka dotted tie and he was smiling and cheerful, just like his old self" (letter to her mother, July 11, 1944, box 9, Lela Mae Stiles Papers).

36. Robert H. Ferrell, ed., *Dear Bess: The Letters from Harry to Bess Truman, 1910–1959*, 509–10.

37. Harry H. Vaughan Oral History, 77.

38. Robert H. Ferrell, ed., "A Visit to the White House, 1947: The Diary of Vic H. Housholder," 326; Ross Diary, April 19, 1946, Ross Papers; Harry S. Truman, *Memoirs: Year of Decisions* (Garden City, N.Y.: Doubleday, 1955), 5.

39. Heaster, interview, 24.

40. Ickes Diary, September 24, 1944.

41. Robert H. Ferrell, *Harry S. Truman: A Life*, 175.

42. "You're the Boss—Reference Material," box 28, Edward J. Flynn Papers.

43. McIntire, *White House Physician*, 204–5. The book relates the terminal date for this condition as November 1. McIntire's files give it as October 4 ("Collier's Article . . . ," box 2, McIntire Papers).

44. Park, *Impact of Illness*, 244.

45. Ward, *Closest Companion*, 348.

46. Ibid., 353. When the president left Warm Springs for Washington on Sunday, December 17, so as to be in the mansion for Christmas, Lucy came aboard the train at Atlanta and left at Augusta.

47. Hassett, *Off the Record*, 304; Ward, *Closest Companion*, 355–56; the blood pressure that follows is from Bruenn, "Clinical Notes . . . ," 304.

48. Ward, *Closest Companion*, 362.

49. Ibid., 364.

Chapter 4: Yalta and Warm Springs

1. Smith Diary, January 4, 1945, "Conferences with President Roosevelt, 1943–1945," box 3, Smith Papers.

2. Ward, *Closest Companion*, 366–67; Jonathan Daniels interview with Leahy, "Notes for *The Man of Independence*," Jonathan Daniels Papers; Ickes Diary, July 16, 1948.

3. For the following see W. C. Heinz, "A Story about Lenny Unfolds," "Lenny Finds a Gift of Magic," and "Lenny Answers a Secret Call," undated, "Roosevelt, Franklin Delano—health," vertical file.

4. Ward, *Closest Companion*, 377–78.

5. Jack McDonald, "Lenny, One-Time SF Fight Manager Treated Roosevelt," undated, enclosed in Creel to McIntire, July 30, 1946, "White House Physician," box 12, McIntire Papers. "Regarding the comment on Mr. Lenny, there is some basis for the article. I did not see Mr. Lenny in action but George Fox did. My understanding is that Miss Suckley had some interest in trying to help him in his efforts to establish himself as a physical therapist or in some similar sort of way in New York. From his long association in the fighting game he was supposed to have developed a special technique in massage of the feet. Just why the President decided to allow him to demonstrate is something that I am not clear on. However, it was perfectly harmless at the time, although in my own estimation poor judgment" (McIntire to Creel, August 2, 1946, "White House Physician," box 12, McIntire Papers).

6. Ward, *Closest Companion*, 378.

7. Frances Perkins, *The Roosevelt I Knew*, 391–94.

8. Tom L. Clark Oral History, 35; George Martin, *Madam Secretary: Frances Perkins*, 461.

9. Anna to John Boettiger, January 26, 1945, "Boettiger, John and Anna, Nov. 1943–Feb. 1945," box 6, John Boettiger Papers.

10. William M. Rigdon, *White House Sailor*, 139.

11. "For your own information, I do know . . . that my father did a great deal of studying of papers and documents given to him by the State Department and other experts in preparation for the Yalta meeting. This studying was done . . . in the privacy of his own quarters. I do not see, therefore, how Mr. Byrnes would have categorical knowledge concerning what my father studied or did not study in preparation for the meeting at Yalta" (Anna Roosevelt Halsted to John L. Snell, December 30, 1955, "Roosevelt, Franklin D.: Correspondence with FDR 1945–1955," box 64, Halsted Papers).

12. According to Elliott Roosevelt, McIntire said that the president's plane should fly low, "Nothing over seven thousand five hundred. And that's tops" (*As He Saw It*, 147). Richard Neuberger, then an Oregon journalist, afterward a U.S. senator, inquired of McIntire, who responded, "Regarding the one point that you have made as to the altitude that President Roosevelt was able to fly without discomfort—there were many times when it was necessary for us to go well above 10,000 feet. On one occasion when flying over the Atlas I suggested oxygen, but we found that he did not need it. There were several other times when we did go above the 10,000-foot level. Very naturally, I preferred not to fly above the 8,000-foot level as

that is always comfortable. I think Elliott must have picked some figures out of the air. It is quite true that Otis Bryan did make a preliminary flight from Cairo to Teheran to see what could be done about flying through the mountain passes. He did an excellent job and as I remember it we did go above 9,000 feet" (letter of January 17, 1947, "White House Physician," box 12, McIntire Papers). Bryan was the president's pilot.

13. William D. Leahy, *I Was There*, 290, 297–98.

14. Campbell and Herring, *Diaries of Edward R. Stettinius, Jr.*, 235; Moran, *Churchill*, 239, 242.

15. Leahy, *I Was There*, 321; Bruenn to McIntire, August 1, 1948, "White House Physician," box 12, McIntire Papers; Park, *Impact of Illness*, 272, 274ff.

16. Charles E. Bohlen, *The Transformation of American Foreign Policy*, 44.

17. "As far as the Soviets were concerned, I do not think Roosevelt had any real comprehension of the great gulf that separated the thinking of a Bolshevik from a non-Bolshevik, and particularly from an American. He felt that Stalin viewed the world somewhat in the same light as he did, and that Stalin's hostility and distrust, which were evident in the wartime conferences, were due to the neglect that Soviet Russia had suffered at the hands of other countries for years after the Revolution. What he did not understand was that Stalin's enmity was based on profound ideological convictions" (Bohlen, *Witness to History*, 211).

18. Herman, "The President's Cardiologist," 12–13; Heaster, interview, 31.

19. February 5, 1945, "Boettiger, John and Anna, Nov. 1943–Feb. 1945," box 6, Boettiger Papers. Not long afterward Anna's husband visited Harold and Jane Ickes in Virginia, and the secretary of the interior wrote, "John has had several letters from Anna and she has spoken of her father as being in good health" (Ickes Diary, February 25, 1945).

20. Jonathan Daniels Oral History, 53.

21. Bohlen, *Witness to History*, 206.

22. McIntire, *White House Physician*, 233–34; Rosenman Oral History, by Jerry N. Hess, 18–19, 38.

23. Robert G. Nixon Oral History, 42–43.

24. Anna to John Boettiger, February 14, 1945, "Boettiger, John and Anna, Nov. 1943–Feb. 1945," box 6, Boettiger Papers.

25. Hassett, *Off the Record*, 318. Daniels said he had never seen him "looking better." He was "in grand spirits; in great shape." A reporter said he took it that Daniels was putting to rest reports from Europe that the president had been ill. "I can set them at absolute rest," Daniels replied. "I have never seen him looking so well" (*New York Times*, March 1, 1945). The

reactions of Hassett and Daniels, to be sure, demonstrated how FDR could look good one day, bad the next.

26. Samuel I. Rosenman, *Working with Roosevelt,* 527.

27. Ward, *Closest Companion,* 400.

28. Marvin Jones Oral History, 122–25.

29. Sidney O. Krasnoff, *Truman and Noyes: Story of a President's Alter Ego,* 38–39.

30. Daniels Oral History, 52–53.

31. King Diary, March 10, 1945.

32. Bohlen, *Witness to History,* 206–7. Engaged in the negotiations with Argentina, Asst. Secy. of State Breckinridge Long believed the president susceptible to bad advice: "But I am not sure now-a-days that things are properly and fully presented to the President and in such manner that he can pass on these matters with a full understanding of the consequences of decisions" (Breckinridge Long Diary, November 1, 1944).

33. Daniels, *White House Witness,* 266. On one occasion when Anna Boettiger went up to the president's bedroom with Daniels the latter saw what she was about. "Anna Boettiger had a very bad cold but she stayed with us and it is becoming increasingly clear that she means to be what the papers are suggesting that she is—a sort of special secretary close to the President, handling details for him and serving as intermediary for others who handle details for him" (Daniels Diary, March 5, 1945, *White House Witness,* 265).

34. Ward, *Closest Companion,* 401; Heaster, interview, 11; notation of March 8, 1967, by Dr. Halsted on a letter from Bruenn, March 1, "Bruenn, Howard G. 1963–1975," box 8, Halsted Papers.

35. Robert H. Ferrell, ed., *FDR's Quiet Confidant: The Autobiography of Frank C. Walker,* 132.

36. Margaret Suckley Oral History, 1.

37. Hassett, *Off the Record,* 327–29.

38. Ibid., 329.

39. Ward, *Closest Companion,* 403.

40. Tully, *F.D.R., My Boss,* 359.

41. Ward, *Closest Companion,* 412.

42. Suckley Oral History, 2.

43. Elizabeth Shoumatoff, *FDR's Unfinished Portrait,* 98.

44. Ibid., 78–79.

45. Shoumatoff believed these were the president's last words (ibid., 117). Daisy Suckley remembered "I have a terrific headache" (Freidel, *Franklin D. Roosevelt,* 605).

46. Herman, "The President's Cardiologist," 13.

Chapter 5: Conclusion

1. Rosenman, *Working with Roosevelt*, 467–69.

2. Ferrell, *FDR's Quiet Confidant*, 125. Sen. John W. Bricker of Ohio was being prominently mentioned for the GOP nomination.

3. Freidel, *Franklin D. Roosevelt*, 513.

4. It seems entirely possible that the president brought the FBI into this case. The reporter Merriman Smith accompanied Roosevelt to South Carolina, found himself virtually excluded from Hobcaw, and at the end of his stay composed an account of the president's vacation that sounded as if he had seen more than he did—he was attempting to justify his expense account. The president read the story and was incensed, thinking Smith had bribed someone at the estate. Press Secretary Early called Smith in and said the president "is going to put the FBI on this thing" (A. Merriman Smith, *Thank You, Mr. President: A White House Notebook*, 142–44). Smith managed to explain his sources.

5. John M. Blum, ed., *The Price of Vision: The Diary of Henry A. Wallace, 1942–1946*, 380; Anna Roosevelt Halsted Oral History, 48. The interviewer asked the president's daughter if she thought her father ever really confided in anybody. "I don't know," was the response. "That's something that I think is one of those questions that is an impossibility to answer, for the simple reason that we don't know his relationship, and never will know, with either Lucy or with Missy LeHand or even his personal relationship with Harry Hopkins. I don't know. I have no idea whether he—I would doubt, I would think that he might have confided to Lucy and Missy, certainly more than he did, I would think, to his children" (50).

6. In great old age Truman spoke about Roosevelt to the writer Thomas Fleming: "He was the coldest man I ever met. He didn't give a damn personally for me or you or anyone else in the world as far as I could see" ("Eight Days with Harry Truman," 56). During his last years the former president was "spacy," his thoughts unreliable, but this is an arresting commentary. To Fleming he added a remark he often made in earlier years: "But he was a great President. He brought this country into the twentieth century" (loc. cit.). Eisenhower recorded a conversation of January 7, 1955, with Sen. Walter F. George of Georgia. The recording was on a dictabelt, and the National Archives transferred it to a tape and released it on March 14, 1997.

7. "Louis Howe was the only one of the official family who called FDR 'Franklin.' It was 'Mr. President' or 'the Boss' for the rest of us" (McIntire, *White House Physician*, 68–69). "Truman, I would say, is easier to work with than Roosevelt was, in the sense that he's a less majestic figure. He's much

more human, and he has more of the characteristics of an ordinary human being. With Roosevelt, you could never forget the majesty of the office, and in a sense the majesty of the person. He was always cordial, affable, but he was never really familiar, except on very rare occasions when he'd go on picnics or when he'd be off on the boat. You never really could forget that this was the President of the United States" (Rosenman Oral History, by James N. Perlstein, 222–23).

8. "But entering into this was Roosevelt's personality, his deep-set conviction that he was the whole cheese. He was, let us face it. This bolsters what I said previously, that I don't believe that it *ever* occurred to Roosevelt that he would die. He had been in the White House twelve years, and I suppose he figured he would have a fifth term. It never occurred to him that anybody else would be President" (Nixon Oral History, 128).

9. Remarks by Dr. Fishman following author's lecture at the college, "The Illness and Death of Franklin D. Roosevelt"; letter to author, September 22, 1997.

10. "[W]hen you say in your manuscript that it was suggested by the consultant group in March 1944 that the President be informed of the seriousness of his health situation: Do you know if he was actually so informed and, if so, what was his response, if any? Did he ask questions, especially those which would relate to prognosis? It occurs to me that McIntire might have informed the group that he would undertake to inform the President, and that as McIntire was both White House Physician as well as Surgeon General, no one queried him as to whether or not he had informed the President and, if he had, what was the President's reaction" (Anna Roosevelt Halsted to Bruenn, October 24, 1969, "Bruenn, Howard G. 1963–1975," box 8, Halsted Papers); interview, August 16, 1958, folder 1, box 15, Richard H. Rovere Papers. "People have . . . said, 'Did he have any idea he was dying?' This I've always been able to say positively, 'No, he didn't, he hadn't the slightest idea.' He was always making plans for the future, what he felt—his tremendous interest in the United Nations and plans for the United Nations, and his plans for going to England the year after the war. He was planning on writing. He had all kinds of projects. No, I don't think he had the slightest idea that he was going downhill in the way he was" (Halsted Oral History, 51).

11. In the literature about Roosevelt it is difficult to discover criticism. The most satisfactory account of his personality appears in the biography by Patrick J. Maney, *The Roosevelt Presence: A Biography of Franklin Delano Roosevelt*. For another shrewd appraisal, see Amos Perlmutter, *FDR and Stalin: A Not So Grand Alliance, 1943–1945:* "The man who appeared so generous with his energy, and so accessible, was also elusive. He was a

friend to the whole world, but intimate with few, if any. He could inspire affection and loyalty, even though he was never really close to any person, not even the mother who adored him and lived her life for him . . . Roosevelt resisted being known because he lacked confidence in the abilities of others" (26).

12. Henry L. Stimson and McGeorge Bundy, *On Active Service in Peace and War,* 581.

Manuscripts

Boettiger, John. Papers. Franklin D. Roosevelt Library, Hyde Park, N.Y.

Bruenn, Howard G. Diary. Franklin D. Roosevelt Library.

Daniels, Jonathan. Papers. Harry S. Truman Library, Independence, Mo.

Davies, Joseph E. Diary. Library of Congress, Washington, D.C.

Early, Stephen T. Papers. Franklin D. Roosevelt Library.

Farley, James A. Diary. Library of Congress.

Flynn, Edward J. Papers. Franklin D. Roosevelt Library.

Hachmeister, Louise. Diary. Box 18, Lela Mae Stiles Papers, Franklin D. Roosevelt Library.

Halsted, Anna Roosevelt. Papers. Franklin D. Roosevelt Library.

Ickes, Harold L. Diary. Library of Congress.

King, W. L. Mackenzie. Diary. Microfiche. University of Toronto Press.

Long, Breckinridge. Diary. Library of Congress.

McIntire, Ross T. Papers. Franklin D. Roosevelt Library.

Morgenthau, Henry A., Jr. Diary. Franklin D. Roosevelt Library.

Rigdon, William M. Papers. Franklin D. Roosevelt Library.

Roosevelt, Franklin D. Papers. Franklin D. Roosevelt Library.

Rosenman, Samuel I. Papers. Franklin D. Roosevelt Library.

Ross, Charles G. Diary. Harry S. Truman Library.

Rovere, Richard H. Papers. State Historical Society of Wisconsin, Madison.

Smith, Harold D. Diary. Franklin D. Roosevelt Library.

Stiles, Lela Mae. Papers. Franklin D. Roosevelt Library.

Suckley, Margaret. Diary. Franklin D. Roosevelt Library.

Truman, Harry S. Papers. Harry S. Truman Library.

Walker, Frank C. Papers. University of Notre Dame, South Bend, Ind.
Watson, Edwin M. Papers. University of Virginia Library, Charlottesville.
Willkie, Wendell. Papers. Lilly Library, Indiana University, Bloomington.

Interviews

Bruenn, Howard G. Interview by author. Riverdale, N.Y., February 16, 1992.
———. Interview by Brenda L. Heaster. Riverdale, N.Y., April 21–22, 1989. Transcript courtesy of interviewer.
———. Interview by Jan Kenneth Herman. Riverdale, N.Y., January 31, 1990. Transcript courtesy of interviewer.

Oral Histories

Clark, Tom L., by Jerry N. Hess. Harry S. Truman Library. 1972–1973.
Daniels, Jonathan, by J. R. Fuchs. Harry S. Truman Library. 1963.
Halsted, Anna Roosevelt, by James E. Sargent. Oral History Collection, Oral History Research Office, Butler Library, Columbia University, New York. 1973.
Jones, Marvin, by Jerry N. Hess. Harry S. Truman Library. 1970.
Nixon, Robert G., by Jerry N. Hess. Harry S. Truman Library. 1970.
Perkins, Frances, by Dean Albertson. Oral History Collection, Oral History Research Office, Butler Library. 1951–1955.
Rosenman, Samuel I., by James N. Perlstein. Oral History Collection, Oral History Research Office, Butler Library. 1959–1960.
———, by Jerry N. Hess. Harry S. Truman Library. 1968–1969.
———, by Joseph Wall. Oral History Collection, Oral History Research Office, Butler Library. 1957.
Suckley, Margaret, by Rexford G. Tugwell. Franklin D. Roosevelt Library. 1957.
Vaughan, Harry H., by Charles T. Morrissey. Harry S. Truman Library. 1963.

Other Sources

Adams, Herbert Dan. *The Knife That Saves: Memoirs of a Lahey Clinic Surgeon.* Boston: Francis A. Countway Library of Medicine, Harvard University Medical School, 1991.

Asbell, Bernard. *When F.D.R. Died.* New York: Holt, Rinehart and Winston, 1961.

Austen, Frank K., Miriam W. Carmichael, and Raymond D. Adams. "Neurologic Manifestations of Chronic Pulmonary Insufficiency." *New England Journal of Medicine* 257 (1957): 579–90.

Bateman, Herbert E. "Observations on President Roosevelt's Health during World War II." *Mississippi Valley Historical Review* 43 (1956–1957): 82–102.

Bishop, Jim. *FDR's Last Year: April 1944–April 1945.* New York: Morrow, 1974.

Blum, John M., ed. *The Price of Vision: The Diary of Henry A. Wallace, 1942–1946.* Boston: Houghton Mifflin, 1973.

Boettiger, John R. *A Love in Shadow.* New York: Norton, 1978.

Bohlen, Charles E. *The Transformation of American Foreign Policy.* New York: Norton, 1969.

———. *Witness to History: 1929–1969.* New York: Norton, 1973.

Breitman, Richard, and Alan M. Kraut. *American Refugee Policy and European Jewry: 1933–1945.* Bloomington: Indiana University Press, 1987.

Bruenn, Howard G. "Clinical Notes on the Illness and Death of President Franklin D. Roosevelt." *Annals of Internal Medicine* 72 (1970): 579–91.

Bumgarner, John R. *The Health of the Presidents: The Forty-one United States Presidents through 1993 from a Physician's Point of View.* Jefferson, N.C.: McFarland, 1994.

Bundy, McGeorge. *Danger and Survival.* New York: Random House, 1988.

Burns, James M. *Roosevelt: The Soldier of Freedom.* New York: Harcourt, Brace, Jovanovich, 1970.

Calhoun, Daniel A., and Suzanne Oparil. "Hypertensive Crisis since FDR—A Partial Victory." *New England Journal of Medicine* 332 (April 13, 1995): 1029–30.

Campbell, Thomas M., and George C. Herring, eds. *The Diaries of Edward R. Stettinius, Jr.: 1943–1946.* New York: New Viewpoints, 1975.

Colville, Sir John R. "The Personality of Sir Winston Churchill." In *Winston Churchill: Resolution, Defiance, Magnanimity, Good Will,* ed. R. Crosby Kemper III, 108–25. Columbia: University of Missouri Press, 1996.

Crispell, Kenneth R., and Carlos F. Gomez. *Hidden Illness in the White House*. Durham: Duke University Press, 1988.

Daniels, Jonathan. *White House Witness: 1942–1945*. Garden City, N.Y.: Doubleday, 1975.

Esfahanian, Kathleen. "A Shadow on the Presidency: Roosevelt's Last Year." Master's thesis, University of Connecticut, 1988.

Evans, Hugh E. "The Medical History of President Franklin D. Roosevelt." Courtesy of author.

Fabricant, Noah B. *Thirteen Famous Patients*. Philadelphia: Chilton, 1960.

Feerick, John D. *From Failing Hands: The Story of Presidential Succession*. New York: Fordham University Press, 1965.

Feingold, Henry L. "Courage First and Intelligence Second: The American Jewish Secular Elite, Roosevelt and the Failure to Rescue." *American Jewish History* 72 (June 1983): 424–60.

Ferrell, Robert H. *Choosing Truman: The Democratic Convention of 1944*. Columbia: University of Missouri Press, 1994.

———. *Harry S. Truman: A Life*. Columbia: University of Missouri Press, 1994.

———. *Ill-Advised: Presidential Health and Public Trust*. Columbia: University of Missouri Press, 1992.

———, ed. *Dear Bess: The Letters from Harry to Bess Truman, 1910–1959*. New York: Norton, 1983.

———. *FDR's Quiet Confidant: The Autobiography of Frank C. Walker*. Niwot: University Press of Colorado, 1997.

———. "A Visit to the White House, 1947: The Diary of Vic H. Housholder." *Missouri Historical Review* 78 (1983–1984): 311–36.

Fields, Alonzo. *My Twenty-one Years in the White House*. New York: Coward-McCann, 1960.

Fleming, Thomas. "Eight Days with Harry Truman." *American Heritage* 43 (July–August 1992): 54–59.

Flynn, Edward J. *You're the Boss*. New York: Viking, 1947.

Flynn, John T. *The Roosevelt Myth*. Garden City, N.Y.: Doubleday, 1948.

Freidel, Frank. *Franklin D. Roosevelt: A Rendezvous with Destiny*. Boston: Little, Brown, 1990.

Gallagher, Hugh C. *F.D.R.'s Splendid Deception.* New York: Dodd, Mead, 1985.

Gellman, Irwin F. *Secret Affairs: Franklin Roosevelt, Cordell Hull, and Sumner Welles.* Baltimore: Johns Hopkins University Press, 1995.

Gilbert, Robert E. *The Mortal Presidency: Illness and Anguish in the White House.* New York: Basic Books, 1992.

Goldberg, Richard T. *The Making of Franklin D. Roosevelt: Triumph over Disability.* Cambridge, Mass.: Abt, 1981.

Goldsmith, Harry S. "Unanswered Mysteries in the Death of Franklin D. Roosevelt." *Surgery, Gynecology and Obstetrics* 149 (December 1979): 899–908.

Goodwin, Doris Kearns. *No Ordinary Time: Franklin and Eleanor Roosevelt, the Home Front in World War II.* New York: Simon and Schuster, 1994.

Halsted, James A. "F.D.R.'s 'Little Strokes': A Medical Myth." *Today's Health* 40 (December 1962): 53, 74–75.

Harding, Warren G., II, and J. Mark Stewart. *Mere Mortals: The Lives and Health Histories of American Presidents.* Worthington, Ohio: Renaissance, 1992.

Hassett, William D. *Off the Record with F.D.R.: 1942–1945.* New Brunswick: Rutgers University Press, 1958.

Herman, Jan Kenneth. *Battle Station Sick Bay: Navy Medicine in World War II.* Annapolis: Naval Institute Press, 1997.

———. "The President's Cardiologist." *Navy Medicine* 81:2 (March–April 1990): 6–13.

Israel, Fred L. *The War Diary of Breckinridge Long: Selections from the Years 1919–1944.* Lincoln: University of Nebraska Press, 1966.

Josephson, Emanuel M. *The Strange Death of Franklin D. Roosevelt: History of the Roosevelt-Delano Dynasty, America's Royal Family.* New York: Chedney, 1948.

Keith, N. M., H. P. Wagener, and N. W. Barker. "Some Different Types of Essential Hypertension: Their Course and Prognosis." *American Journal of Medical Science* 197 (1939): 332–43.

Kitchens, James H., III. "The Bombing of Auschwitz Reexamined." *Journal of Military History* 58 (April 1994): 233–65.

Krasnoff, Sidney O. *Truman and Noyes: Story of a President's Alter Ego.* West Palm Beach, Fla.: Jonathan Stuart, 1997.

Leahy, William D. *I Was There.* New York: Whittlesey House, 1950.

L'Etang, Hugh. *The Pathology of Leadership*. New York: Hawthorn, 1970.

Littell, Norman M. *My Roosevelt Years*. Ed. Jonathan Dembo. Seattle: University of Washington Press, 1987.

Looker, Earle. "Is Franklin D. Roosevelt Physically Fit to Be President?" *Liberty* (July 25, 1931): 6–10.

MacMahon, Edward B., and Leonard Curry. *Medical Cover-Ups in the White House*. Washington, D.C.: Farragut, 1987.

Maney, Patrick J. *The Roosevelt Presence: A Biography of Franklin Delano Roosevelt*. New York: Twayne, 1992.

Martin, George. *Madam Secretary: Frances Perkins*. Boston: Houghton Mifflin, 1976.

Marx, Rudolph. *The Health of the Presidents*. New York: Putnam, 1960.

Matzozky, Eliyho. "An Episode: Roosevelt and the Mass Killing." *Midstream* 26 (August–September 1980): 17–19.

McCune, William S. "Malignant Melanoma: Forty Cases Treated by Radical Resection." *Annals of Surgery* 130 (September 1949): 318–32.

McIntire, Ross T. "Did U.S. Elect a Dying President?: The Inside Facts of the Final Weeks of FDR." *U.S. News and World Report* 30 (March 23, 1951): 19–22.

———. "They Keep You Fit to Fight." *Shipmate* 6 (August 1943): 14–15, 80–81.

———. *White House Physician*. New York: Putnam's, 1946.

Messerli, Franz H. "This Day Fifty Years Ago." *New England Journal of Medicine* 332 (April 13, 1995): 1038–39.

Miller, Nathan. *FDR: An Intimate History*. Garden City, N.Y.: Doubleday, 1983.

Moran, Lord (Charles Wilson). *Churchill: Taken from the Diaries of Lord Moran: The Struggle for Survival, 1940–1965*. Boston: Houghton Mifflin, 1966.

Morgan, Ted. *FDR: A Biography*. New York: Simon and Schuster, 1985.

Newton, Verne W., ed. *FDR and the Holocaust*. New York: St. Martin's, 1996.

Nicholas, H. G., ed. *Washington Despatches, 1941–1945: Weekly Political Reports from the British Embassy*. Chicago: University of Chicago Press, 1981.

Park, Bert E. *Ailing, Aging, Addicted: Studies of Compromised Leadership.* Lexington: University Press of Kentucky, 1993.

———. *The Impact of Illness on World Leaders.* Philadelphia: University of Pennsylvania Press, 1986.

Parks, Lillian Rogers, and Frances Spatz Leighton. *The Roosevelts: A Family in Turmoil.* Englewood Cliffs, N.J.: Prentice-Hall, 1981.

Perkins, Frances. *The Roosevelt I Knew.* New York: Viking, 1946.

Perlmutter, Amos. *FDR and Stalin: A Not So Grand Alliance, 1943–1945.* Columbia: University of Missouri Press, 1993.

Post, Jerrold M., and Robert S. Robins. *When Illness Strikes the Leader: The Dilemma of the Captive King.* New Haven: Yale University Press, 1993.

Reilly, Michael F. *Reilly of the White House.* New York: Simon and Schuster, 1947.

Rigdon, William M. *White House Sailor.* Garden City, N.Y.: Doubleday, 1962.

Roosevelt, Elliott. *As He Saw It.* New York: Duell, Sloan and Pearce, 1946.

———. *Eleanor Roosevelt, with Love: A Centenary Remembrance.* New York: Dutton, 1984.

———, ed. *F.D.R.: His Personal Letters.* 3 vols. New York: Duell, Sloan and Pearce, 1947–1950.

Roosevelt, Elliott, and James Brough. *Mother R.: Eleanor Roosevelt's Untold Story.* New York: Putnam's, 1977.

Roosevelt, Franklin. *Complete Presidential Press Conferences of Franklin D. Roosevelt.* 25 vols. New York: Da Capo, 1972.

Roosevelt, James, and Sidney Shalett. *Affectionately, FDR: A Son's Story of a Courageous Man.* New York: Harcourt, Brace, 1959.

Roosevelt, James, with Bill Libby. *My Parents: A Differing View.* Chicago: Playboy Press, 1976.

Rosenman, Samuel I. *Working with Roosevelt.* New York: Harper, 1952.

Rosenman, Samuel I., and Dorothy Rosenman. *Presidential Style: Some Giants and a Pygmy in the White House.* New York: Harper and Row, 1976.

Rubinstein, William D. *The Myth of Rescue: Why the Democracies Could Not Have Saved More Jews from the Nazis.* New York: Routledge, 1997.

Shoumatoff, Elizabeth. *FDR's Unfinished Portrait*. Pittsburgh: University of Pittsburgh Press, 1990.

Smith, A. Merriman. *Thank You, Mr. President: A White House Notebook*. New York: Harper, 1946.

Smith, Richard Norton. *Thomas E. Dewey and His Times*. New York: Simon and Schuster, 1982.

Stimson, Henry L., and McGeorge Bundy. *On Active Service in Peace and War*. New York: Harper, 1948.

Thorne, Christopher. *Allies of a Kind: The United States, Britain and the War against Japan, 1941–1945*. New York: Oxford University Press, 1987.

Trohan, Walter. *Political Animals: Memoirs of a Sentimental Cynic*. Garden City, N.Y.: Doubleday, 1975.

Tully, Grace. *F.D.R., My Boss*. New York: Scribner's, 1949.

Walch, Timothy, ed. *At the President's Side: The Vice Presidency in the Twentieth Century*. Columbia: University of Missouri Press, 1997.

Ward, Geoffrey C. "FDR's Twenty-Four-Year War." *American Heritage* 36:4 (June–July 1985): 14, 16.

————, ed. *Closest Companion: The Unknown Story of the Intimate Friendship between Franklin Roosevelt and Margaret Suckley*. Boston: Houghton Mifflin, 1995.

Wold, Karl C. *Mr. President—How Is Your Health?* St. Paul and Minneapolis: Bruce, 1948.